THE MULTICULTURAL MIND

THE
MULTICULTURAL
MIND

Unleashing the Hidden Force for
Innovation in Your Organization

DAVID C. THOMAS

BK

Berrett–Koehler Publishers, Inc.
a BK Business book

Berrett-Koehler Publishers, Inc.
1333 Broadway, Suite 1000
Oakland, CA 94612-1921
Tel: (510) 817-2277 | Fax: (510) 817-2278 | www.bkconnection.com

ORDERING INFORMATION
Quantity sales. Special discounts are available on quantity purchases by corporations, associations, and others. For details, contact the "Special Sales Department" at the Berrett-Koehler address above.
Individual sales. Berrett-Koehler publications are available through most bookstores. They can also be ordered directly from Berrett-Koehler: Tel: (800) 929-2929; Fax: (802) 864-7626; www.bkconnection.com.
Orders for college textbook/course adoption use. Please contact Berrett-Koehler: Tel: (800) 929-2929; Fax: (802) 864-7626.
Orders by US trade bookstores and wholesalers. Please contact Ingram Publisher Services: Tel: (800) 509-4887; Fax: (800) 838-1149; E-mail: customer.service@ingram publisherservices.com; or visit www.ingrampublisherservices.com/Ordering for details about electronic ordering.

Berrett-Koehler and the BK logo are registered trademarks of Berrett-Koehler Publishers, Inc.

Printed in the United States of America.

Berrett-Koehler books are printed on long-lasting acid-free paper. When it is available, we choose paper that has been manufactured by environmentally responsible processes. These may include using trees grown in sustainable forests, incorporating recycled paper, minimizing chlorine in bleaching, or recycling the energy produced at the paper mill.

Library of Congress Cataloging-in-Publication Data

Names: Thomas, David C. (David Clinton), 1947–
Title: The multicultural mind : unleashing the hidden force for innovation in your organization / David C. Thomas.
Description: First Edition. | Oakland : Berrett-Koehler Publishers, Inc., 2016. | Includes bibliographical references and index.
Identifiers: LCCN 2015035792 | ISBN 9781626561014 (pbk.)
Subjects: LCSH: Diversity in the workplace. | Organizational change.
Classification: LCC HF5549.5.M5 T46 2016 | DDC 658.4/063—dc23
LC record available at http://lccn.loc.gov/2015035792

FIRST EDITION

21 20 19 18 17 16 | 10 9 8 7 6 5 4 3 2 1

Produced and designed by BookMatters, edited by Mike Mollett, proofed by Janet Blake, indexed by Leonard Rosenbaum, and cover designed by Brad Foltz

CONTENTS

PREFACE

Recent research has confirmed something that we have suspected for a long time—multicultural experience leads to greater creativity. People who have multiple cultural identities (multiculturals) are at the top of the list of people with significant multicultural experience. In this book I marry this new research with well-known findings from psychology and management to create a road map for understanding this growing segment of the workforce, the multicultural mind, and how organizations can leverage and model people with these unique skills to produce innovative organizations. The principles of innovation are not a secret, but the secret weapon in achieving innovation in your organization may be the multicultural mind.

While grounded in sound scientific research, this book is not an academic text. It is a guide for understanding the potential of a newly emerging and significant portion of the workforce that may hold the key to innovation for many companies. Unlike many management books, this book does not offer simple "back of the envelope" solutions to complex problems. Rather, I try to synthesize the existing knowledge about multiculturals and innovation in a way that managers will find useful. By understanding multicultural individuals and modeling their development, organizations can chart a course for innovation that takes advantage of a resource that has been hidden in plain sight, the multicultural mind.

The book is divided into three parts. Part 1 introduces multicultural individuals and describes how the same forces of globalization that have created the complex and dynamic environment in which organizations must compete have also provided a resource to help them compete: multicultural individuals. Part 1 also describes the sources of cultural identity; how growing up in a particular society shapes the way we think and behave, and how multiculturals internalize two or more sets of values, attitudes, and beliefs about appropriate behavior. Finally, part 1 describes the process of confronting cultural differences that results in a multicultural mind. This can occur in many ways, from moving to a new country to dealing with culturally different coworkers.

Part 2 is devoted to developing the kind of understanding of multiculturals that is required to engage with them effectively in organizations. I discuss the many ways in which multicultural individuals experience and manage their multiple cultural identities, and the implications that this has for them, their social relationships and for how their unique skills (broader worldview, heightened sensitivity and perceptual acuity, greater empathy, and greater cognitive complexity) can best be utilized. I also discuss the relationship of multilingualism to multiculturalism and the role that language plays in managing a culturally diverse workforce. Finally, I show how visible differences in individuals influence the way in which multiculturals see themselves and the world, as well as how they can help with strategies for managing dissimilar groups in organizations. The categorization of people according to surface characteristics can mask the value that they bring to organizations.

In part 3 I focus on what organizations can do to leverage the unique skills of multiculturals in the service of innovation. I discuss how important the work situation is in influencing multiculturals and on the process of innovation, and what organizations can do to create the type of climate (flexible situations, strong communication, and sufficient resources) that is needed. Understanding how the work situation fosters or supresses innovation is a key factor in leveraging the skills of multiculturals. I also outline the roles (bridging, integrating, mediating) that multiculturals can play to get the most out of multicultural teams, which we have long known are a source of creative ideas. Finally, I offer some ideas on developing organizations that allow multiculturals to assume roles in which they can best contribute to innovation. I also show how modeling the experience of multiculturals can lead to everyone developing a multicultural mind.

This book asks us to think differently about managing diversity in organizations. The multicultural mind is the product of the diversity that exists within individuals, as opposed to between individuals. Understanding the value of a multicultural mind is a significant step in creating organizations that work for and bring out the best in everyone.

ACKNOWLEDGMENTS

A number of individuals and organizations have contributed to the production of this book. I am very grateful to Steve Piersanti, Jeevan Sivasubramaniam, Neal Maillet, and everyone at Berrett-Koehler for caring about the book and making it the best it can be. It was a pleasure to again work with David Peattie at BookMatters, and I thank Mike Mollett for his expert and sensitive copyedit. Rebecca Buckwalter-Poza, Jim Wylde, and Silvia Brugge provided comments on an early draft of the manuscript. This was very helpful, and I am grateful. I am very thankful for the flexibility that was allowed me in my positions with the Beedie School of Business, Simon Fraser University, and the Australian Business School, University of New South Wales to engage in this type of work. In addition to the academic research referenced, the book was influenced by the numerous discussions I have had on this topic with my colleagues, most notably Mary Yoko Brannen, Stacey Fitzsimmons, and Andre Pekerti. Finally, not only was my partner, Lisa, supportive of this work, she read and commented on every chapter. Her perspective as a multicultural person as well as her attention to detail greatly improved the manuscript.

Part I

INTRODUCING MULTICULTURALS

The Multicultural Mind and Innovation

CHAPTER ONE

A RESOURCE HIDING IN PLAIN SIGHT

Multiculturals and Innovation

There was a time when all an organization needed to succeed was to improve. But in today's dynamic and complex competitive environment organizations need to innovate, and most of them know it. What many don't know is that there is a largely untapped source of innovation that is hiding in plain sight. These are individuals with multiple cultural identities,[1] such as:

> Carlos Ghosn, born in Brazil to Lebanese parents, educated in France, and is now a superstar CEO in—Japan? He is so famous for turning around the fortunes of Nissan that his life story has been made into a Japanese comic book series. He is the CEO of Renault-Nissan Alliance.

> Ralph Baer (born Rudolph Heinrich Baer in Germany) immigrated to the United States with his family as a result of World War II. He took up electronics and trained as a radio service engineer. In the 1960s he came up with the idea of playing games on television screens and went on to develop the Magnavox Odyssey and other consoles and game units. Known

as the "Father of Video Games," he was awarded the National Medal of Technology in 2004.

Arianna Huffington was born in Greece, moved to the United Kingdom at age 16, and was educated at Cambridge University. Her early life after university involved traveling to music festivals for the British Broadcasting Corporation and spending summers in France. After moving to the United States, she developed a career as an author and syndicated columnist. One of the most influential women in media, she is president and editor in chief of The Huffington Post Media Group.

Muhtar Kent was born in New York City in 1952. His father, Necdet Kent was the Turkish consul general. He attended high school in Turkey and then earned undergraduate and MBA degrees in the United Kingdom. He is chairman and CEO of the Coca-Cola Company.

What these highly successful individuals all have in common of course is their multicultural backgrounds. However, what may be more important to their success is that their multicultural experience has allowed them to perceive and process information differently. They have *multicultural minds!*

The flattening of the world through globalization has given more and more people the opportunity to have multicultural experiences. For example, more than 13 percent of Americans were born outside the United States, and in Canada and Australia immigrants make up more than 20 percent of the population.[2] Migrating to a new country, having parents from different cultures, or spending a significant amount of time in a foreign country has become commonplace. However, these multicultural experiences do not always lead to having a multicultural mind. These individuals may not have developed multicultural identities, or they may have difficulty in managing their identities. Or they may never have been in situations that allowed their multicultural identities to come to the surface. Ghosn, Baer, Huffington, and Kent have been fortunate in that their multiculturalism allowed them to develop multicultural minds, and their environment allowed them to leverage their unique skills and abilities. Not everyone is this fortunate. This book is about understanding how multicultural experience leads to a multicultural mind, how organizations can leverage this ability in their employees for competitive advantage, and how each of us can develop a multicultural mind.

The Multicultural Mind and Organizations

To understand, engage, and learn to harness the skills of individuals with multiple cultural identities, we must challenge several assumptions about managing cultural diversity in today's organizations.

First, as a result of globalization, it is now commonplace that employees and managers in organizations are multicultural. They have internalized the values, attitudes, beliefs, and assumptions about behavior of more than one culture. Therefore, focusing on managing the differences *among* individuals with unique cultural profiles must be tempered with an understanding of how to help individuals manage the cultural differences that exist *within* themselves.

Second, when we understand that individuals can internalize more than one cultural profile, we challenge the assumption that any sort of visible surface indicator can provide effective insight into an individual's cultural makeup. Organizations must get to know their employees at a deeper level.

Finally, much of what has been published about managing diversity has focused on gaining knowledge about culturally different others and building on that knowledge to bridge cultural differences. This book is not about bridging differences. It is about using difference to advantage. It is about leveraging the skills that individuals with multiple cultural identities bring to the organization and also using their special skills and abilities to grow the organization.

Today's organizations need to *innovate* not only to succeed but (for many) just to survive. Some management scholars such as Gary Hamel argue that it is a nonlinear, nonobvious, nonincremental type of innovation that will produce long-term competitive advantage.[3] However, there are many types of innovation, all of which might be important to organizations. The first, which Hamel is talking about, is a radical change to products and services that can dramatically alter what companies do. Examples include the automobile, penicillin, the laptop computer, the iPad, and online shopping. A second type is a radical change to processes. These changes in fundamental ways to manage, design, produce, or distribute are rare. Some examples are the automobile production line and the Six Sigma approach to error reduction.[4] A third type involves incremental improvement in products, services, or processes. Most innovations are of this type and lead to developments such as cost reduction, product enhancements, improvements in environmental or safety performance. Examples include the second-generation iPad, same-day dry cleaning, and reductions in the amount of water used in the production of food. The Conference Board defines innovation as "the process through which economic and social value is extracted from knowledge through the generation, development, and implementation of ideas to produce new or improved strategies, capabilities, products, services, or processes."[5] At the center of this definition of innovation is the word *ideas*. The generation, development, and implementation of new and improved ideas occurs when individuals have expertise, are motivated, and most important think differently.[6] Of course new ideas are founded on factual knowledge and technical expertise. We wouldn't expect innovation in gene splicing or computer software to come from someone without significant expertise in those areas. Likewise, just because people are capable of generating creative ideas does not mean they will do so. They must have the desire, the motivation to put forth the effort. We have long known that intrinsic motivation (deep interest, involvement, curiosity, and enjoyment of the work itself) is the most powerful driver of creativity.[7]

In the following story, Ruth not only has the knowledge and motivation to be creative, but she has the ability to see things that others have missed and to *think differently*.

Ruth Marianna Moskowicz was born in Denver, Colorado, to Polish-Jewish immigrants. She married Elliot Handler, a businessman and inventor who cofounded Mattel Toys in 1945. While Elliot invented toys for the fledgling company, Ruth Handler stayed at home raising their two children, Barbara and Kenneth. When Barbara was a preteen in the early 1950s, Ruth noticed her playing with paper dolls as if they were adults. At the time the only three-dimensional dolls on the market were made to look like babies, not adult women. Ruth mentioned her idea of a three-dimensional doll shaped like an adult woman (with a wardrobe made out of fabric) to her husband and to Harold

Matson, the other cofounder of Mattel. Both men rejected the idea, believing that parents would not buy their children a doll with a voluptuous figure. But on a trip to Switzerland, Ruth discovered a German doll with an adult figure and fashion wardrobe called a "Bild Lilli Doll," which was designed after a cartoon character and originally marketed to adults in bars and tobacco shops as a gag gift. She redesigned the doll and named it after her daughter. "Barbie" debuted at the New York toy fair in 1959.[8]

New ideas come from creative thinking. There are numerous definitions of creativity, but the following ones capture the essence of creativity and of a creative person:

Creativity is the production of novel and useful ideas in any domain.

A creative person is one who has insight, who can see things nobody else has ever seen before, who hears things nobody has heard before.[9]

There was a time when we thought that creativity was the domain of a few gifted individuals. That may have been true in some instances in the past, but Stanford professor and IDEO (the global design company) partner Diego Rodriguez cautions us to be wary of the "lone inventor myth" in today's world.[10] We now know that creativity in organizations is most often the result of multiple inputs and that creativity in groups and individuals can be developed and nurtured.[11]

The following story tells how an environment encouraged people to think differently and how it contributed to one of the most influential innovations of our time.

It was October 7, 1957, and physicists William Guier and George Weiffenbach were engaged in deep discussion in the cafeteria of the Applied Physics Laboratory (APL) of Johns Hopkins University. They were talking about the announcement over the weekend of the launch of *Sputnik 1*, the first artificial satellite. They wondered if anyone at APL had managed to capture (with the lab's equipment) the signal the Soviets had engineered into the satellite. After determining that no one had, they used a radio wave analyzer and a tape recorder to capture the 20 MHz signal. They had included time stamps with each recording and realized they could use the Doppler effect to calculate the speed at which the satellite was moving. (The Doppler effect is the predictable way the frequency of a wave changes when its source is in motion. You can hear the Doppler effect when a vehicle with a siren moves past you and the sound slides down in pitch.) As word spread around the APL, a steady stream of scientists came by Weiffenbach's office to hear the electronic beeps. Because *Sputnik* was emitting a steady signal and the receiver was stationary, Guier and Weiffenbach realized that they could calculate the movement of the satellite and ultimately its track. In the following weeks, a loose network of scientists helped fill in the details on orbiting bodies and refine the theory. With the use of one of the early computers, a UNIVAC, they were able to plot a complete description of *Sputnik*'s orbit based on the simple 20 MHz beeps. In the spring of 1958, Frank McClure, then director of APL, asked the men confidentially if they could reverse the question; as opposed to calculating the exact position of a satellite from a fixed position on the ground, could they calculate the position of a receiver on the ground if they knew the position of the satellite? Within a few days Gruier and Weiffenbach had solved the inverse problem. It turns out that McClure had good reason for asking the question as the military was developing the Polaris nuclear missiles, and they needed to know the precise location of submarines in order calculate accurate trajectories for the missiles. The system, called Transit, was developed by the new APL Space Department and allowed the Navy to steer its ships using satellite technology. In 1983 President Ronald Reagan declared that satellite navigation should be a common good and opened it up to civilian use. Now, almost 60 years after the development of Transit, there are 68 satellites in the GPS system, which allows ships and airplanes to navigate to their destinations and you and me to locate the nearest coffee shop with our mobile phones.[12]

In designing Transit, Guier and Weiffenbach had the expertise and intrinsic motivation to come up with a creative solution. They also enjoyed an environment of collegial collaboration that gave them an extra boost, something that I discuss in more detail in the chapters ahead. While both expertise and motivation are important elements of creativity, the most exciting new developments have been on the creative thinking component of creative performance. We have recently come to understand that an important way in which creative thinking develops is through significant multicultural experience, that is, experience with other cultures leads to more creativity.

In 2009 Will Maddux and Adam Galinksy published the report of an experiment that showed empirically that experience in a foreign country leads to creativity.[13] Their study was inspired by the widely held assumption that a period of living abroad was required for the development of aspiring artists. This assumption was based on anecdotal evidence such as Hemingway's penning of *The Old Man and the Sea* in Cuba, and that much of Gauguin's best work was inspired by living in Tahiti, or the fact that Handel composed the *Messiah* while living in England and many other such stories.

The experiment involved 205 MBA students of whom 66 percent had lived in a foreign country and 98.5 percent had traveled abroad. The students were given a creative task called the Duncker candle problem in which they were shown a picture containing several objects on a table: a candle, a pack of matches, and a box containing tacks.[14] The problem is to figure out how to attach the candle to the wall by using all the objects on the table so that it burns properly and does not drip wax on the table or the floor. The correct solution requires the participant to empty the box of tacks, use the tacks to attach the box to the wall, and use melted candle wax to attach the candle to the box. The problem requires creative thinking in that it involves the ability to consider objects as performing other than their usual function (the box as a candle holder as opposed to a receptacle for tacks).

Of the 205 students, 111 solved the problem correctly. More importantly, the study found a positive relationship (after controlling for such things as age, gender, and nationality) between the amount of time individuals had *lived* in a foreign country and their ability to solve the problem correctly. However, it found a negative relationship between time spent *traveling* abroad and the ability to come up with a creative solution.

This experiment tells us that while multicultural experience leads to creativity, it doesn't do so for everyone and for every type of multicultural experience. Not everyone who travels to a foreign country, even for an extended period of time, develops the multicultural mind required for creative performance. Unfortunately, it's more complicated than that. That brings us back to the likes of Ghosn, Baer, Huffington, and Kent and the seemingly almost automatic way in which these multicultural individuals developed a multicultural mind.

Multiculturals

Multiculturals are individuals who identify with more than one culture. They have been exposed to and taken on board the values, attitudes, beliefs, and assumptions about appropriate behavior of multiple cultures. This occurs naturally in individuals who grow up in multicultural families, where their parents are from two different cultures, or when an individual grows up in two or more different cultures. Some multiculturals (Ghosn, Baer, Huffington, and Kent for example) are able to manage their multiple identities successfully and take advantage of the multicultural minds they have developed over time. However, others (discussed in chapter 4) do not manage their conflicting identities well and are not able to take advantage of their unique skills and abilities. Understanding that there is not one type of multicultural person is an important starting point for organizations that want to get the most from this growing demographic. In 2010 Wayson Choy, a Chinese Canadian novelist, gave a keynote speech on multiculturalism in Canada. In his speech Choy described multiculturals as being like composite materials. These materials are used in particular types of manufacturing because they are lighter, stronger, cheaper, or more flexible, which makes them particularly well suited to their specific task.

However, they require much work to develop. Like composite materials, multicultural individuals may have skills and abilities that are particularly well suited to the global business environment, but they need help to recognize and develop these skills, and they must be well matched to their organizational roles.[15]

Multiculturals in Organizations

Much research and practice regarding the management of diversity in organizations assumes that individuals have only one cultural profile. For example, we have been concerned with the issue that Hispanics and Anglos might have a different orientation to time or that Asians and westerners might view hierarchy and power relationships differently. Understanding these differences and how they affect behavior is important.[16] However, once we recognize the presence of multiculturals in organizations, we are presented with an entirely new way of thinking about cultural diversity. Realizing that cultural diversity exists within individuals as well as within organizations challenges many of our assumptions about managing diversity at the organizational level and also presents opportunities for organizational development. The most important issues for multiculturals may not be the conflict that exists between groups but the conflict among the values, attitudes, beliefs, and assumptions about appropriate behavior that exist within themselves.[17]

Organizations must foster cultures in which the diversity that exists *within* individuals is recognized in the same way that we have come to treat cultural diversity *between* individuals as a valuable asset. This means that these culturally complex individuals are integrated into knowledge-sharing and decision-making systems. We must help them to develop and then use their multicultural minds to help organizations come up with the creative solutions they need.

Creativity and innovation are not the same things. The most creative idea that is not implemented does not result in innovation. The creative spark that allowed Ruth Handler to recognize the potential in the Barbie doll came to fruition only after she saw the development of a similar idea in a foreign context and gained acceptance from the founders of Mattel. Innovation requires the ability to see problems in new ways and to know which ideas are worth pursuing. But it also requires the ability to sell other people on the value of the idea.[18] Organizations can benefit from multicultural minds, as we've seen in the APL example, only if they provide opportunities for the creativity of multiculturals to be unleashed and for them to assume appropriate roles in the process of innovation. Organizations must understand multiculturals and engage with them in order to create an environment that leverages their unique skills and abilities and then model the multicultural experience for all employees.

Summary

The forces of globalization that have created the superheated competitive environment that organizations now face have also provided a resource to address the problem. The flattening of the world has given more people the opportunity to experience other cultures, as a result of both migration and growing up in a multicultural environment. As a result, there are many more people with multicultural identities in today's organizations. This significant experience with other cultures is important because it leads to more creative thinking. Creative thinking, along with appropriate expertise and intrinsic motivation, are the key components of creative performance. However, to achieve innovation creative ideas must not only be generated, they must be implemented. Both the generation and implementation of creative solutions to problems requires that organizations find ways to leverage the unique talents of their multiculturals and their culturally diverse workforce. To do this they must understand the multicultural mind and create an environment where it can reach its full potential. Understanding the multicultural mind begins with understanding the influence of culture on individuals. That is the subject of the next chapter.

CHAPTER TWO

WHY MEXICANS SPEAK SPANISH

Sources of Cultural Identity

The continuing existence of different languages and cultures around the world might seem out of step with the homogenizing forces of globalization. However, culture and our cultural identity have a profound influence on how we think, feel, and act. The history of how cultures develop helps us understand the persistence of cultural influence and the importance of multiculturals.

Before the European discovery of what is now Mexico, a small number of shipwrecked sailors showed up on the shores of the Yucatán Peninsula. One of these was a Castilian named Jerónimo de Aguilar. After narrowly escaping being the featured actor in a Maya ritual sacrifice, de Aguilar and another shipwreck survivor, Gonzalo Guerrero, escaped into the interior, where they encountered a friendlier tribe (they were both enslaved, but at least they hadn't been eaten). Both de Aguilar and Guerrero assimilated into the Maya culture—learning the language and adopting Indian ways; Guerrero took a Maya wife who bore him two children. Eight years later, Hernán Cortés made several brief forays into the Yucatán and learned of his countrymen's existence. Guerrero and de Aguilar reacted to Cortés's arrival in different ways. Guerrero, completely Mayanized, refused to join his countrymen and was later killed while fighting on the side of the Indians against the Spaniards. De Aguilar, by contrast, was pleased to be reunited with his countrymen, and Cortés ransomed him from his Indian captors for a few glass beads. Regardless of his initial reasons for contacting his countryman, Cortés soon came to realize that de Aguilar's knowledge of the language and culture of the Maya could be invaluable in his quest for gold. The rest, as they say, is history; the invasion of the Spanish changed the language, religion, and many aspects of culture of this part of the world. Without the multicultural skills of de Aguilar, things might have turned out differently.[1] There are numerous other examples of a culture being affected by colonization. However, there is perhaps no better example of how the skills of a multicultural individual influenced the process of cultural development. While cultures continue to evolve, they are deeply woven into the fabric of the society.

All societies must develop ways to deal with three fundamental issues. The first issue is the preservation of the society itself. For example, societies set up mechanisms to defend themselves from threats both real and imagined.

The second issue is the nature of the relationship between the individual and the group and the coordination of social interaction. For example, people in many Western cultures shake hands with their right hand as a form of greeting. Initially, this was probably an indication that no weapon was being held or about to be drawn with the dominant right hand. Similarly, the

Maori of New Zealand have an elaborate challenge ceremony or *wero,* which involves sending forth warriors who challenge the visiting party by prancing about and brandishing fighting weapons followed by presenting a token on the ground to their leader, to determine the intentions of visitors. Having determined the intent of a visitor, there is no need in this culture to display an empty right hand as a form of friendly greeting. As a sign of peace, the Maori greeting among individuals is to press noses, or *hongi.*[2]

The third issue is the relationship of people to the natural world. Societies are made up of people—biological organisms that must deal with basic issues such as food and protection from the elements. Evidence of the response of society to the natural world is found in the delightful variety of cuisines around the world that have their basis in the availability and preference for certain ingredients. Societies have developed different ways of solving these three fundamental issues because of differences such as climate, geography, the indigenous economy, and interaction with other societies. This is the source of culture.

Culture

Over time, societies have developed (sometimes elaborate) sets of values, attitudes, and assumptions about appropriate behavior that are associated with being a member of that society. This cultural knowledge is passed on from one generation to the next. Guidance about behavior that is considered appropriate in a particular culture is often contained in the stories that parents tell their children, such as those about societal heroes.[3] For example, people in the United States know that the story of George Washington's life demonstrates honesty because of his willingness to accept the consequences of chopping down a cherry tree by confessing to it. People in Saudi Arabia know to be kind to spiders because they protected the prophet Muhammad by hiding him from his enemies. People in China know to honor their teachers on September 29 to celebrate the anniversary of the birth of Confucius. This knowledge has a long-lasting effect because it is learned, often at an early age, in terms of fundamental beliefs about the way we should behave or the goals to which we should aspire. This is why cultural differences continue to exist in the face of the homogenizing effects of globalization.

A side effect of the creation of cultural groups with fundamental beliefs about how things should be or how we should behave is the attitude of *ethnocentrism*. Ethnocentrism is the belief that one's own cultural group is the center of everything and all other groups are evaluated with reference to it. Ethnocentric beliefs include the following:

- What goes on in our own culture is seen as natural and correct, and what goes on in other cultures is unnatural and incorrect.

- We perceive our own cultural customs as universally valid.

- We unquestionably think that our cultural norms, roles, and values are correct.

- We believe that it is natural to help and cooperate with members of our own culture, to favor and feel proud of them, and to be distrustful and even hostile toward members of other cultures.[4]

This categorization of *them* and *us* is a natural process of the formation of different cultural groups, and it underlies many of the issues facing the world today.

The persistence of cultural differences around the world does not mean that cultures are completely resistant to change. On the contrary, some aspects of culture are influenced by modernization. In today's society all people may need to possess a core set of psychological characteristics to survive.[5] In modern postindustrial societies, most people spend their productive time interacting with people and symbols, with a growing emphasis on self-expression and autonomous decision making. Therefore, to survive in this modern context, people may need to have a sense of personal efficacy, an egalitarian attitude toward others, an openness to innovation and change, independence or self-reliance, and high achievement motivation.[6] While the demands of modern society may blur some cultural differences, it is important not to apply the notion of a convergence of cultures too broadly. The case of the McDonaldization of the world provides an example. The seemingly identical McDonald's restaurants that exist almost everywhere actually have different meanings and fulfill different social functions in different parts of the world. Although the physical facilities are similar, eating in a McDonald's is a different *social* experience in Japan or China or the United States or France.[7] In the same way, what it means to be modern can take on different forms in different societies.

Culture is more than a random assortment of customs. It is an organized system of values, attitudes, beliefs, and behavioral meanings that are related to one another, to a society's physical environment, and to other cultural groups. It is often very hard to understand facets of culture outside their cultural context. For example, Americans believe that people should take responsibility for themselves and not rely on others.[8] However, the United

States has the highest percentage of charitable giving in the world, and Americans readily volunteer their time to help with community projects and in emergencies. This seeming paradox is explained by recognizing the requirement to help those in need that was forged on the American frontier.[9] Under normal circumstances Americans believe that one should take personal responsibility and not rely on others. However, some situations can overwhelm individual initiative and ingenuity and require the help of others. Therefore, not only are these cultural traditions not contradictory, they are logical when considered in the context of how American culture developed.

People often talk about the values associated with a culture. Values, which are beliefs about what ought to be or how one should behave, are *consciously* held in the sense that they are explanations for the observable features of culture. For example, Chinese people work hard because they were taught that people *should* work hard. The ultimate source of these values is the basic underlying assumptions, which are shared by the culture, and which are held deeper in people's knowledge. These basic ways of reacting to the world shape beliefs, perceptions, thoughts, and feelings at an *unconscious* level and are taken for granted by members of a cultural group; therefore, the effects of culture are often not apparent to a society's members and are often overlooked. For example, Americans may not know why it is normal to give to charity or to volunteer in an emergency; they just know this is the way it is. And the act of bowing as a way of communicating with others is so deeply ingrained in Japanese people that they are often seen bowing to the unseen partner in a telephone conversation. Three things about culture are important to remember:

1. Culture is the meanings that are shared by members of society—a social group.

2. These cultural meanings are learned from previous generations.

3. Language is an especially important artifact of culture that helps to perpetuate the culture and shapes the way people view the world.[10]

Understanding that culture is associated with social groups has important implications for the emergence of multicultural individuals as a key component of the workforce. First, our membership in a cultural group helps to determine how we perceive ourselves—our self-identity—as well as how others perceive us. Second, groups have systems of norms and expectations about appropriate behavior that give them stability despite changes in their membership. However, the characteristics of groups can in fact change as key members or large numbers of members come and go as indicated by the Spanish influence in Mexico. The circumstances that ripped de Aguilar and Guerrero from their Castilian culture are of course unusual and dramatic. However, migration across cultural boundaries has been occurring for all of human existence, and the forces of globalization have made the boundaries to such migration permeable.

The current magnitude of migration is large indeed. According to the Global Commission on Migration, there were nearly 200 million migrants in 2005, counting only those who have lived outside their country for a year or more. This is equivalent to the population of the world's fifth-largest country—Brazil. Economic opportunity is a big driver of migration. For example, up to 20 percent of the total population of New Zealand has migrated to live and work outside their country.[11] Two recent trends in migration are worth noting. First, the number of women migrants is increasing. In 1976 fewer than 15 percent of migrants were women, while in 2005 more than half were females.[12] Second, the traditional migration pattern following World War II was the flow of low-skilled workers from less developed to more developed countries. Today's migrants are much more likely to be highly skilled.

Migrating to a new country is a dramatic event, as the following immigrant stories suggest:

> I didn't know much at the time, as it all happened so fast. I knew my parents were trying to get us to Canada, but the actual move happened within a couple of weeks. To be honest, I was scared because, I hate to admit it, but I was one of those people who thought Canada was a country full of snow, ice and igloos. I was convinced I would have to dogsled to school. . . . When I first joined my swim club, Toronto Swim Club, I could barely speak a word of English, but being in a team allowed me to interact and pick up the language within months with the help and patience of my team. I was dropped into a new country and new environment, which is a hard thing to deal with, but the pool became a place for me where I knew people and people knew me. It was a familiar environment in an unfamiliar world. (Hungarian born Canadian Olympic swimmer Zsofia Balazs)[13]

> I was born in Freetown, Sierra Leone. There was a war in my home country, so we had to leave. When I was six, my family was living in a refugee camp in Liberia, which is a country that neighbors Sierra Leone. We were picked by some officials there to come to America. I was really sad because I had to leave my family and friends; I will not get to see them again until I am grown and can go back to Liberia as an adult. Leaving was hard,

but my mom made me feel better by telling me that in America we would learn to use the telephone to keep in touch. Now, I can call my family and talk to them by phone. They speak Mende, and I speak English to them to help them learn my new language, too. (Vandi, age 12, now living in the United States)[14]

We had to deny our Polish heritage in order to become German as quickly as possible. During my childhood, many Germans still had negative views of Poland, and I wanted to have nothing to do with it. At home, my parents spoke Polish, but I spoke back to them in German. German officials changed my name: from Alicja to Alice. Within a year, I learned to speak German without an accent. Many years later, at the age of 16, I went to the United States for a year as an exchange student. Being Polish didn't carry the same baggage there as it did in Germany. People just said, "Oh, great!" That was totally new to me. It was an important step that led me to decide to reclaim my second half, my Polish identity. (Polish-born German author Alice Bota)[15]

All immigrants have a unique personal story. The way in which an individual responds to the new environment will be specific only to them, because each individual has personality characteristics that are shared by no one else. Extroverts may be more likely to seek out new friends in the foreign culture, and individuals who are open to new experiences may feel less threatened by the differences they encounter. However, regardless of personality, age, country of origin, or the country to which they migrated, and regardless of their economic status, their stories have a consistent theme. It is a search for their identity—how they fit into the new and strange environment in which they find themselves. Of course, in many cases this means learning a new language as well. The process of adjusting to a new cultural environment is called acculturation.

Acculturation

Acculturation involves the psychological and behavioral changes that people experience because of contact with another culture. Typically, it is used to describe the changes in people who relocate from one culture to another, such as Guerrero and de Aguilar, in the story that opened this chapter. However, acculturation can also occur on a larger collective scale when a whole group, as opposed to the individual, changes (e.g., the large group of Turkish immigrants in the Netherlands or the nation of Japan when controlled by the United States after World War II).[16] The gradual process of psychological acculturation that occurs during immigration results in changes in individual behavior, identity, values, and attitudes.[17] Guerrero, in addition to acquiring a Maya wife, also acquired, among other things, Maya facial tattoos and holes in his ears for ornaments. However, his shipmate de Aguilar assimilated somewhat less to the Maya culture. The acculturation patterns of individuals and groups can be influenced by a number of individual differences and situational factors. The status of individuals, their facility in communicating in the local language, their personality, and whether the immigrants forge relationships with host country nationals or with coethnics (people like themselves) are all factors that influence acculturation patterns. For example, recent research found that individuals who formed initial close relationships with coethnics had a strong tendency to adhere to their culture of origin, while those who (like Guerrero) formed initial close relationships with host nationals showed a stronger tendency to adapt to the new culture.[18]

Adapting to a new culture is not easy. The severe disorientation that people feel when experiencing an unfamiliar way of life is called *culture shock* and results from the absence of a familiar language and cues to appropriate behavior.[19] It's somewhat like waking to find the landscape covered with new-fallen snow in which everything familiar has disappeared. Trying to find one's way without familiar landmarks can cause uncertainty and stress. Navigating a new culture with its different set of attitudes, beliefs, and assumptions about appropriate behavior is equally disconcerting.

For some people adjustment to the new culture is successful. Guerrero met a romantic partner in the new environment. Some people's view of the new country becomes so positive that they lose all desire to return home, like Mike in the following story:

> As he looked out from the top-floor restaurant over Lake Michigan and the magnificent Chicago skyline, Yukimichi (Mike) Kusumoto thought about how his expatriate assignment to the United States had turned into a permanent move. Intially, like many Japanese, he had great difficulty adjusting to the extreme foreignness of the United States. The crime rate statistics were so frightening that he came to Chicago without his wife Naoko and his children, intending to accomplish his assignment and then return to his firm back in Japan. However, what was even more frightening when he arrived was the amazing diversity in America. The sheer variety of people and cultures in Chicago was startling. At the office, he had initially been frustrated by the shortsightedness of his colleagues, their failure to treat customers as "honored guests," and their use of

lawyers to protect them from their own hasty decisions. Yes, adjusting to the United States had been difficult.

He couldn't say exactly when he began to feel more comfortable here in Chicago than back in Tokyo. Of course his English was now very good, and Naoko had joined him after a year and had eventually integrated well into American society. By carefully observing and trying to understand the American business practices, he had finally been very successful—so successful that a competing company had eventually headhunted him to a much higher salary. Even though he had insisted that his two daughters go to the special Japanese school in the Chicago suburb where they lived, they were now as American as they were Japanese—not a bad thing, he thought. Now he expected that they would attend an American university rather than go back to Japan. For himself Yukimichi had grown to appreciate the American way of life. He enjoyed its freedoms and spontaneity and loved his spacious home and beautiful neighborhood—such a contrast with the tiny apartment he had left in Tokyo. He had even found himself admiring the independence of Americans, and he did his best to act that way himself. It seemed to suit his personality. Go back to Japan? No, he was an American now.[20]

Some individuals with experience living in multiple cultures acculturate to the extent that they demonstrate the ability to function effectively in more than one culture. But not everyone does, and not everyone becomes multicultural as a result. Time living in another culture or through intensive daily interaction with people who are culturally different develops cultural flexibility so that people can adjust their behavior based on the cultural context of the situation. Becoming multicultural involves more than just adopting the behavioral patterns of another culture; it means internalizing aspects of the other culture at a deep level.

Summary

Today, we are all in contact with individuals who identify with cultures different from our own, and often with more than one culture. The result of changing migration patterns and national differences in birth rates, coupled with other boundary-spanning aspects of globalization, is changing the nature of the workforce in most of the world. More and more individuals in organizations have multicultural experience, and many are multicultural. In order to take advantage of their multicultural minds to create innovation in organizations, we must first understand multicultural individuals. A first step in that understanding is recognizing that the cultural values, attitudes, beliefs, and assumptions about appropriate behavior are programmed at a deep level. We learn these things as a result of being members of a cultural group. We learn them at a young age from our parents or others who influence us. While this mental programming can change through acculturation, it is resistant to change. The way in which culture is learned makes it invisible, sometimes even to members of the culture. Like the invisible jet streams that guide the path of weather systems, culture has a powerful hidden influence on behavior.[21] Multicultural individuals are different because they have internalized two, or sometimes more, sets of these cultural frameworks that guide their lives. To develop a multicultural mind, they must be able to hold different conceptions of themselves reflecting these different cultural assumptions. How this occurs is the subject of the next chapter.

CHAPTER THREE

SOMETIMES I FEEL LIKE A MOTHERLESS CHILD

How Confronting Cultural Differences Results in a Multicultural Mind

The phrase "sometimes I feel like a motherless child," from the traditional African American spiritual, reflects the search for a sense of place and of self by the slaves who were transported from their African homeland. The song expresses the pain and despair of this longing. The questions Who am I? and Where do I belong? are central to understanding multicultural persons. How individuals come to experience another culture is perhaps less important than the act of confronting another culture on an existential level. Confronting cultural differences is critical to developing a multicultural mind.

As noted in chapter 2, some individuals will have accultur-ated as a result of migration. Others will have grown up in a multicultural family where they learned to identify with more than one culture. Still others will experience one culture in part of their lives (e.g., at work or school) and another culture in a different part of their lives (e.g., at home). Individuals who spend a significant part of their childhood growing up in one or more foreign cultures (often as the sons or daughters of foreign service employees, missionaries, or expatriates) are such a well-known example of multiculturals that they have been named third culture kids (TCKs).

The key to developing a multicultural mind is the experience of dealing with the different values, attitudes, beliefs, and assumptions about appropriate behavior that are contained in their multiple cultures. As a result of this exposure, multicultural individuals must consciously consider who they are, often on a regular basis. The experience of author Malcolm Gladwell (*The Tipping Point, Blink, Outliers*) is not uncommon. Gladwell was born to an English father and Jamaican mother and recalls an incident at a high school track meet, when a West Indian team member observing him curiously asked, "*What* are you?" He remembers being overwhelmed by the word *what,* as it signified to him that it set him apart from blacks as well as whites. He says, "My mother never had to think about whether she was Black. She was. I have to think about it, and turn the issue over in my mind, and gaze in the mirror and wonder, as I was so memorably asked, *what* am I."[1]

All of us think of ourselves as physically distinct. This is our outer self that is visible to others. However, we also have an inner or private self that consists of thoughts and feelings that cannot be known by others.[2] This *self-identity* can consist of personality traits such as competence, attractiveness, and conscientiousness, but it is also shaped by personal experiences. Our concept of self is detailed and complex, as we have a great deal of experience with ourselves. While some aspects of the self-identity are probably a universal aspect of being human, others are specific to different cultures. For example, people in Western cultures are typically expected to think and act as autonomous individuals with unique attributes. Their notion of self is *independent* of others. In contrast, people in many Asian cultures think of themselves as less differentiated and more connected to a particular group of people. Their sense of self is *interdependent* with others. For example, the word for *self* in Japanese, *jinbun,* refers to one's share of the life space.[3]

Adopting a particular self-identity is not simply a matter of choice that is easily changed, but it is deeply programmed. Recent brain-imaging research shows that particular sections of the brain are activated differently by some tasks and social situations depending on whether the person has been brought up in a culture that supports an independent or interdependent self-concept.[4] Our concept of who we are, our self-identity, can have a powerful influence on our behavior. Consider the following experiment:

Participants were asked the probability that they would engage in the following behaviors with members of the following groups: family, friends, coworkers, neighbors, and fellow countrymen.

Suppose you disagreed with many of the members of one of the groups mentioned above about something very important. What are the chances you would confront them and bring the disagreement out in the open?

Suppose you and your spouse or your children are having a problem that is quite embarrassing (e.g., sexual difficulties or heavy drinking). What are the chances you would inform members of the groups mentioned above?

Suppose you notice that many members of the groups mentioned above have a lifestyle that is unhealthy (they smoke, drink, and do other things in excess; they do not exercise enough). What are the chances you would do something about it?

Suppose a member of one of the groups mentioned above got seriously sick, requiring someone to spend a lot of time (40 hours per week) with him or her. What are the chances you would do it?

Suppose a member of one of the groups mentioned above asked you for a loan (about a week's wages). Assume that you have that much in the bank. What are the chances you would lend the money?[5]

Participants with an *interdependent* sense of self were much more likely (about 80 percent probability) to engage in the behavior than those with an *independent* self-concept (about 50 percent probability).

Path to a Multicultural Mind

We once thought that individuals had to give up their existing self-identity in order to take on a new one. We now know that this is not true. People can hold multiple versions of their self-identity that have formed because of their exposure to different cultures. These identities can be either ascribed (involuntary, for example as a result of being raised by culturally different parents) or acquired (chosen, for example as a result of migrating to a different culture). In both cases, however, the path from being exposed to a different culture and developing a multicultural mind is the same. It involves *knowledge* of another culture, *identification* with that culture, *internalization* of the values and attitudes of the culture, and a conscious *awareness* of their multiple cultural identities.[6]

Cultural Knowledge. Knowledge of another culture is a prerequisite to identifying with it: you can't identify with a culture without knowing about it. For those who grew up in a single culture, knowledge can be gained in numerous ways, including from books, films, television, and casual contact with other cultures. However, this explicit and superficial knowledge does not provide a basis for a multicultural mind. For westerners, going to a Chinese restaurant is certainly an experience with another culture; however, it provides little insight into Chinese culture. What is needed is a deep involvement with another culture in order to understand its values, attitudes, beliefs, and assumptions about appropriate behavior. By gaining this type of knowledge, individuals can map themselves onto the terrain of the other culture, and their knowledge of the other culture is developed sequentially. For individuals who grew up in multiple cultures, such as TCKs, their knowledge of multiple cultures was gained automatically. They had no choice in the matter.

Cultural Identification. The social part of our identity comes from the groups to which we belong. For example, I might identify with my profession or with my classmates at the school I attended, or any other group of people. We identify with these groups because it makes us feel good to do so or because we are seen as members of the group by ourselves or others. If your skin is a particular shade or you speak with an identifiable accent, others may categorize you as a member of the group to which that characteristic belongs, whether you like it or not. However, you may not necessarily see yourself as a member of that group.

> I never asked to be white. I am not literally white. That is, I
> do not have white skin or white ancestors. I have yellow skin
> and yellow ancestors, hundreds of generations of them. But
> like so many other Asian Americans of the second generation,
> I find myself now the bearer of a strange new status; white,

by acclamation. Thus it is that I have been described as an "honorary white," by other whites, and as a "banana," by other Asians. Both the honorific and the epithet take as a given this idea: to the extent that I have moved from the periphery and toward the center of American life, I have become white inside. Some are born white, others achieve whiteness, still others have whiteness thrust upon them. (Eric Liu, *The Accidental Asian*[7])

One important social group that influences the development of our identity is our cultural group. We all need to understand where we fit in relationship to other people in society. Our collective experience with our cultural group is one way we do that. The knowledge that we belong to a cultural group combined with the value and emotion associated with that membership is an important element of who we are. The extent to which we identify with our cultural group depends in part on how positive we feel about being a member of that group.[8] We all want to feel good about who we are, and identifying with high-status or prestigious groups is one way we do that. Those with exposure to multiple cultures may not identify equally with each culture and may manage their multiculturalism differently.

Cultural Internalization. Identification with multiple cultures has an effect on our attitudes and behavior only if the values, attitudes, beliefs, and assumptions associated with that culture are internalized.[9] Just because I see myself as a member of a particular group does not mean that my attitudes and behavior are guided by the norms of that group. As a fan, I might identify with my favorite sports team and be disappointed when they lose. I might even say "we" in reference to the team. However, that does not mean that my behavior reflects the values of the team or necessarily contributes to their goal of winning. In contrast, my internalization of the values of my cultural group is an important motivator. For example, if I have internalized the cultural value that people should work hard, it will motivate me to be a hard worker, and I will be more likely to work hard. Or if I have internalized the belief that time is a valuable commodity and should not be wasted, I am more likely to be punctual and to become irritated when others are late. For those who have internalized multiple cultures, which culture influences their attitudes and behavior depends on the situation.

Recent research shows that multiculturals can move between their multiple cultural identities depending on the situation. In an example of this research, Hong Kong and Chinese American multiculturals, who possess both East Asian and Western cultural meaning systems, were exposed to either American cultural cues (pictures of the American flag, Superman, Marilyn Monroe, the US Capitol) or Chinese cultural cues (pictures of a Chinese dragon, Stone Monkey, a Peking opera singer, and the Great Wall).[10] The participants were then asked to interpret a photo showing a single fish swimming in front of a group of fish. Those who had been exposed to the American cultural cues were likely to say that the one fish was being influenced by some internal characteristic (independence, personal objective, or leadership), while those exposed to the Chinese cultural cues attributed the fish's behavior to being influenced by the group (being chased, teased, or pressured by others). The reasons given for the fish's behavior were consistent with which cultural meaning system was triggered by the cultural cues (independence for the American cues and interdependence for the Chinese cues). So depending on the situation, the attitudes and behavior of multiculturals can be influenced by either, or any, of their internalized cultural meaning systems.[11] This research will come as no surprise to multiculturals who have experienced this phenomenon.

Cultural Awareness and the Multicultural Mind. Individuals may have more than one culturally based meaning system and switch between cultures based on the situation, but do this automatically without conscious thought as shown in the preceding example. The final stage in the development of a multicultural mind is the *conscious* consideration of the multiple meaning systems that people have in their minds and resolving the differences between them. It is the act of confronting and resolving the potentially different values, attitudes, beliefs, and assumptions about appropriate behavior that results in mental development.[12] What happens is that the internalization of two or more cultures creates the opportunity for conflict between the norms and values of the two (or more) different cultures. In order to resolve these conflicts, people must become consciously aware of them; this allows them to consider the merits of the alternative perspectives and form reasonable trade-offs among them. The increased effort required to resolve these cultural conflicts results in a more complex way of thinking (called cognitive complexity). As described in chapter 2, cultural meaning systems are deeply embedded, and resolving differences requires considerable mental activity, which results in these much more complex thinking patterns. This is how the multicultural mind is formed.

Types of Cultural Integration

Just because someone has been exposed to multiple cultures does not mean he or she will develop a multicultural mind.

Unfortunately, it's not as simple as that. It depends on how individuals respond to this exposure. While there is an infinite range of possible responses, they can be classified into four basic types depending on their stage on the path to a multicultural mind.[13] These types are *cosmopolitans, sympathizers, chameleons,* and *multiculturals.*

Cosmopolitans. Through their exposure to multiple cultures some individuals gain significant knowledge and a sophisticated understanding of other cultures. However, despite having a deep understanding of another culture, these people maintain their cultural independence by identifying with and internalizing only one culture. They may know a lot about other cultures, but their attitudes and behavior are driven by a single cultural meaning system.

Sympathizers. A second type of cultural integration is represented by those individuals who identify with more than one culture but have not internalized the values, attitudes, and behavioral assumptions of a second culture. These individuals may have a psychological attachment to more than one culture and perhaps even think of themselves as having membership in multiple cultures. However, like cosmopolitans, their behavior is guided by a single cultural meaning system. For example, individuals who have lived much of their adult lives in a country other than that of their birth, and may even have taken out citizenship in the new country, can identify with their adopted country, but still not have internalized its values.

Chameleons. People with knowledge of another culture and the ability to mimic the associated behavioral norms can be called cultural chameleons. Just because someone is able to adopt the behavior of more than one culture does not mean that they identify with that culture, or that they have internalized its values. For example, the ability to speak a foreign language does not necessarily reflect an identification with or commitment to the values of a second culture. Talented mimics may give a convincing impression that they belong to a cultural group without any psychological attachment or commitment to that group.

Multiculturals. Truly multicultural individuals have knowledge of, identify with, have internalized and consciously consider the multiple meaning systems that they have in their minds. They are actively involved in resolving the differences between these different cultures. As discussed in the next chapter, they may manage these conflicting identities in various ways. However, the act of confronting and resolving their multiple identities results in a level of mental development not shared by those who have not reached this level of integration. This active and conscious consideration of their multiple selves is what gives these individuals a multicultural mind.[14]

Multicultural Experience and the Multicultural Mind

As noted in chapter 1, not all individuals who have multicultural experience develop a multicultural mind. Multicultural experience provides the opportunity for individuals to become multicultural. However, all multicultural experiences are not the same, and individuals respond differently to these experiences based on how different the cultures are and because of a host of individual differences, including, importantly, their age.

The development of a multicultural mind by integrating two

(or more) cultural meaning systems depends in part on the extent to which the cultures involved are different. If the two cultures are similar to each other and individuals can function effectively using one cultural identity, they are not likely to be motivated to expend the mental effort to resolve minor discrepancies. If the cultures are extremely different, integrative solutions may be just too hard to figure out, and individuals will resort to alternatives to integration such as evasion, procrastination, or rigid coping responses.[15] Therefore, the ideal context in which to develop a multicultural mind is exposure to a culture that is different enough to be challenging yet not so different as to be overwhelming. Of course, individuals can develop a multicultural mind in challenging contexts, but the effort required to do so may be very large indeed.

An important difference in how individuals respond to the challenges of multiple cultures is their age when they are exposed to a new cultural context. We know from developmental psychology that it is during adolescence (11–16 years of age) when youth are struggling with who they want to be and how they wish to be perceived by others.[16] This is the prime time for young people to explore their cultural heritage and identity, to ask questions about their cultural ancestry, and to try to understand what it means to be part of their culture. They may also question choices made by previous generations. For example, first-generation immigrants and former slaves have often concealed their culture and tried to blend in to a dominant culture. However, as later generations consider their cultural identity, they may reclaim their cultural heritage and become active in cultural activities, even resurrecting abandoned cultural symbols. An example is the black is beautiful movement in the United States, which began with a fashion event in 1962 and was originally subtitled "The Original African Coiffure and Fashion Extravaganza Designed to Restore our Racial Pride and Standards."[17]

If exposure to other cultures occurs before individuals resolve their sense of self-identity, the development of their sense of self is influenced by more than one cultural context. This is common in third culture kids (TCKs) like Tim in the following story:

> Born in New York City to a pianist and an international development official for the US government, Tim spent most of his childhood traveling to foreign countries. He spent time in Zimbabwe, India, and Thailand. His interest in amateur photography during high school at the International School of Bangkok took him to Cambodia. He graduated from Dartmouth College and earned a master's degree from Johns Hopkins University. He worked as a consultant for Kissinger and Associates, then the International Affairs division of the Treasury Department as an assistant financial attaché for the US Embassy in Tokyo and then as under secretary of international affairs. In 2001 he moved to the International Monetary Fund, and in 2003 he became the president and chief executive officer of the New York Federal Reserve Bank and served as the vice chairman and permanent member of the Federal Open Market Committee, the group responsible for formulating US monetary policy. On November 25, 2008, Timothy Franz Geithner accepted president-elect Barack Obama's nomination to serve as the 75th secretary of the treasury, where he would play a key role in the management of the financial crisis that began that year.

Third culture kids are unique in that they move between cultures before they have had the opportunity to fully develop their personal and cultural identity.[18] While they have developed the expanded worldview, cross-cultural enrichment, and creativity associated with a multicultural mind,[19] not all TCKs turn out to be as apparently well adjusted as Tim Geithner. These multiculturals can also experience confusion with regard to their values, have difficulty adjusting to adult life, and have a sense of cultural homelessness. The various ways in which individuals manage their multiple identities is the subject of the next chapter.

Summary

People become exposed to other cultures through migration, growing up in a multicultural family or foreign country, and at work or school. As a result of this exposure, they have the opportunity of developing a multicultural sense of themselves, their self-identity, and a multicultural mind. The path from exposure to different cultures to becoming multicultural involves acquiring knowledge of the values, attitudes, and behavioral assumptions of another culture. More important, it involves making this knowledge a part of oneself by identifying with the culture and internalizing its beliefs. Individuals who consciously consider the similarities and differences among their multiple meaning systems, and work to integrate them, develop more complex ways of thinking—a component of a multicultural mind. Individuals differ in how they respond to multicultural experience, especially with regard to their age at the time of second culture exposure. The characteristics of the different cultures to which they are exposed also matters. The ideal situation is one in which the cultures are different enough to be challenging but not so different as to be overwhelming. Once their multiple identities are developed, individuals might adopt a number of strategies to manage them. Understanding the path to the development of a multicultural mind and the various ways that individuals manage their multiculturalism are important steps in understanding the relationship of multicultural experience to innovation, and how we all might develop a multicultural mind.

Part II

UNDERSTANDING MULTICULTURALS

Their Skills and How They See Themselves and the World

CHAPTER FOUR

NEORICANS, MEXICAN AMERICANS, AND CATALAN SPANISH

The Many Ways in Which Individuals Experience and Manage Their Multiculturalism

Not every multicultural understands his or her cultural identity in the same way. In a recent study, a group of researchers asked multicultural individuals what it was like to be multicultural. Many of them responded that it was like being a salad with all the different colors and textures of their cultures combined in one bowl. However, there were many different responses, such as the following:

> I'm like a spice rack. So, different spices and I'm really unique. I do believe, I think I'm different. I do think differently. And like a spice rack, I pick which part of each culture that I would like. And it can change from day to day. (ARAB AMERICAN)

> I think I am probably kind of like the fusion food . . . kind of mix. (CHINESE CANADIAN)

> It's like a game of volleyball, I feel like. Sometimes volleyball can be like calm or you can have like a nice, like a nice, calm game. And sometimes it can get really intense and competitive,

and sometimes I feel like the two cultures, they're balanced.
And sometimes I feel like they're not where it's like competitive
between the two cultures . . . sometimes I feel it's hard to
incorporate the two cultures, just trying to find a way to make
a mix sometimes is difficult. And sometimes I feel like, oh,
it's doable or it's good, it's OK. You can mix the two cultures.
(ARAB AMERICAN)

Kaleidoscope, . . . if you rotate a kaleidoscope you can see
different patterns. You rotate again, you see different patterns,
but they are the same fields, same things which make these
patterns, that take different shapes and show different things.
So what I said is that I—being different cultures, and not only
Indo-American, but within Indian culture also we have different
cultures. (INDIAN AMERICAN)

I am like an oil drop in this water. Even though I am there, with
all this around me, I am still keeping my identity, very separate
from what is around me. But at the same time, I am with all that,
so you know, I think that's what I am, I still have my own very
intact with what I am, but I am still around with everything and
go with that. (INDIAN AMERICAN)[1]

Multicultural individuals must make sense of who they are
in the face of two or more (sometimes very different) meaning systems. The ways in which these individuals organize or
manage their multiple identities varies greatly as the preceding
metaphors suggest. For multiculturals, the organization of their
multicultural mind has implications not only for themselves and
their social relationships but also for how their talents can best be
used in the organization.

A simple way to think about this mental organization is in
terms of the number of cultural identities a person is concerned

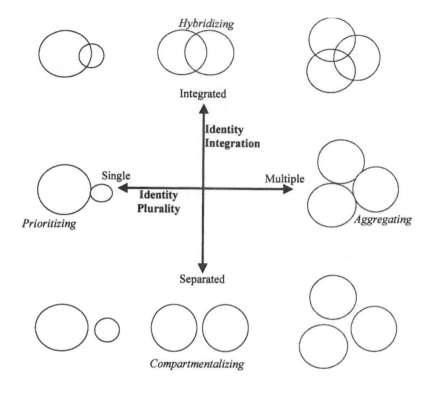

Figure 4.1
Multicultural patterns
(Source: Fitzsimmons, 2013)

with (plurality) and the extent to which these identities are integrated[2] as opposed to kept separate.[3] Taken together, these two dimensions of *plurality* and *integration* produce a map of multicultural patterns as shown in figure 4.1.

As shown in the figure, one person might prioritize one of their cultures over the other, while another person sees their multiple cultures as separate, but equal. While many possible patterns of mental organization exist, combining the two dimensions creates four typical patterns. These are *prioritizing, com-*

partmentalizing, hybridizing, and *aggregating.* The particular pattern that a person uses to make sense of their identity depends in part on their personality. However, both the way in which their multiple identities were formed, their personal history, and the characteristics of the cultures themselves have an influence. For example, a third culture kid trying to reconcile different Japanese and American cultural meaning systems will likely have a different pattern from an American who moved to Canada as an adult.

Prioritizing Pattern

> Since I've spent two thirds of my life in my home country I feel more Slovak than Canadian. The values I was brought up with are rooted deeply within me and I try to keep them and not change. (SLOVAKIAN CANADIAN)

> I still see myself as Sri Lankan. Even if I live here, I belong to Sri Lanka. It is really important to my identity. (SRI LANKAN CANADIAN)[4]

The prioritizing pattern of making sense of multiple cultural identities is typical of first-generation migrants and those who have been exposed to one or a few cultures during the formation of their identity. They are less likely to integrate aspects of the *new* culture into their identity unless they have a very strong requirement to identify with a high-status new culture or to disassociate with their country of origin. Immigrants to North America from Iran are often heard to refer to themselves as Persian, which may be motivated by a belief that this will be viewed as more positive than Iranian. In countries with strong multiculturalism policies, the pressure to integrate one's identity is somewhat diminished. In people with a prioritizing pattern, the two cultural meaning systems are often very different, making them difficult to integrate. Also, individuals with a prioritizing pattern are likely to have grown up in so-called tight cultures where there are very clear norms for behavior and sanctions for those who deviate from those norms.[5] Prioritizing one cultural meaning system reduces uncertainty about how to think and behave. Often people with this pattern of sense-making will describe themselves in terms of a dominant culture, as in "I'm a Japanese living in America."

Compartmentalized Pattern

> I choose one set of norms and behaviors for one situation and perhaps a different one for a different situation. If I find myself in a situation where people from two different cultures interact, I take on the role of translator, even if the language is a common one. (MEXICAN CANADIAN)

> The way to live is entirely different in Indonesia and Canada, and I think there is no "right" way, and it all depends on who you are and where you live. (INDONESIAN CANADIAN)[6]

The compartmentalized pattern is similar to the prioritizing pattern in that the influence of multiple cultures is not integrated. However, one culture is not prioritized, and the influence of these different meaning systems is relatively equal. This is often described as one cultural frame influencing the person in some situations, and the other cultural frame in other situations. This pattern is typical not only of immigrants but also of those who have been raised in one cultural context at home while having extensive contact with another culture at school or work. Large differences in the characteristics of the different cultures are also typically present in these cases. Multiculturalism policies that encourage cultural segregation and a history of friction between the cultures also encourage this pattern. People with this pattern of sense-making typically described themselves in the hyphenated form, as in—"African-American."

Hybridizing Pattern

> I see myself as being a proud Canadian but equally as proud in my Filipino heritage. I don't feel conflicted, confused, or dominated by one group. I only see myself as both—leveraging from experiences and knowledge from one side to bring out the best in another. (FILIPINO CANADIAN)[7]

> I say that I have a relatively stable "blended" or fused Catalan-Spanish identity. I often jokingly label myself as "*xarnega,*" a formerly derogatory term used to describe immigrants to Catalunya coming from other parts of Spain and their children. (CATALAN SPANISH)[8]

The hybrid pattern of organizing cultural identities is characterized by a high degree of integration of cultural meaning systems often resulting in a blended or fusion identity. For example, Neoricans, individuals of Puerto Rican heritage living in New York, identify not with American or Puerto Rican culture but with their fusion culture. This pattern is more common when the cultural influences have some similarity and when there is not a high degree of friction between the cultures. People with this pattern are likely to be second-generation immigrants or those raised in a multicultural family. Policies that reduce cultural segregation support this identity pattern, as do culturally *loose* societies in which a wide variety of behavior is considered normal. These individuals often say that they identify with their hybrid culture but not with either of the underlying cultures. As is the case with Neoricans, they sometimes have a special name for this hybrid identity.

Aggregating Pattern

> I see myself as a wayfarer kind of thing. That's necessarily part of who we are. We may not describe ourselves that way, but that is I guess a modern global citizen. (Indian American)

> A member of many cultures and a broader global culture. (AMERICAN NEW ZEALANDER CANADIAN)[9]

Those individuals with significant exposure to a wide range of cultural meaning systems may develop an aggregating form of multiculturalism. This pattern is characterized by limited integration of several cultural systems. Typically these people will have been raised with a foundation in one cultural system (often a *loose* culture) but also with a variety of cultural influences. Many third culture kids, described previously, have this pattern. In this case, no one culture has a dominant effect on thinking or behavior. Both a large number of cultural influences and a high degree of difference among them contribute to this pattern of sense-making. While people with this pattern see many cultures as valuable parts of their identity, they often have difficulty talking about a specific cultural identity and often use terms such as "citizen of the world" to describe themselves.

Dividing patterns of cultural identity into these four simple types does not mean that multiculturals are equally divided among the four patterns or that other combinations of integra-

tion and plurality do not exist. Wide variation in the way multiculturals make sense of their identity is possible, with cultural
identities uniquely represented within each person.[10] However,
because we all have a desire for consistency in the way we think
about ourselves, integrated identity patterns may be more desirable for many people, as the following example illustrates:

> At home, my parents applauded my ability to speak English as
> well as any American and yet not be an American. In public, I
> carried myself as the representative of a family most of whose
> members didn't speak English well but harbored no greater
> dream than to be Americans. I both hoped and feared that
> sooner or later I would be found out. The public would discover
> that my parents had no desire to become Americans, while my
> parents would realize that I didn't know how or what it meant
> to be Vietnamese in America. I could translate sentences from
> one language to another and back again: tell my mother what
> my teachers said, ask the sales clerk for what my father wanted.
> Within our family, I could live life in our small apartment as
> though it were a distant outpost of Vietnam. Yet every time I
> turned on the television or stepped out of the house, my parents
> and Vietnam seemed far away, otherworldly. I had been rowing
> back and forth, in a relentless manner, between two banks of
> a wide river. Increasingly, what I wanted was to be a burning
> boat in the middle of the water, visible to both shores yet
> indecipherable in my fury. (Lê Thi Diem Thúy)[11]

Implications of Identity Patterns

The ways in which multiculturals make sense of their cultural
identities have implications for themselves as individuals, for

their social relationships, and, importantly, for how their talents can best be used in organizations. Juggling multiple identities is not easy, and the more of them there are and the more different they are, the harder it is. The process of resolving the potentially conflicting systems of meaning associated with different identities can result in personal distress and anxiety, because it creates uncertainty about self-identity (Who am I?). In addition, some individuals feel guilty as a result of prioritizing one set of beliefs over another. By choosing one set of meaning systems over another, they may feel that they have violated their own internal standards. The psychological toll resulting from the bundle of negative emotions associated with managing multiple identities can be high, particularly in cases where the multiple cultures are very different.[12] Those individuals who employ identity management strategies that reduce uncertainty, such as prioritizing and integrating patterns, are likely to experience lower levels of these negative emotions. On the other hand, when individuals have been able to deal effectively with differences in their multiple meaning systems and/or draw on the enhanced mental ability this creates, they can experience positive emotions and even learn to enjoy their multiple identities.[13]

Individuals who successfully manage the psychological toll associated with managing their multiple identities have the opportunity to use their membership in multiple cultural groups to advantage. They are often better connected across multiple groups because they are more likely to include people from different cultures in their social network. As a result, they are better able to act as boundary spanners and develop positive relationships across culturally different groups. The relationships they develop often result in higher levels of trust, respect, and a sense of mutual obligations. This so-called social capital facilitates interactions by encouraging cooperation.[14]

As indicated previously, the process of finding a pattern with which to make sense of multiple cultural influences is stressful, but it can also have a positive influence on social relationships. In addition, the way in which an individual organizes their multicultural mind influences the skill set they bring to organizations. One obvious outcome of having significant exposure to multiple cultures is an expanded worldview.

The ability to bring a variety of perspectives to problems is an often observed characteristic of multiculturals, as the management of L'Oréal has discovered. L'Oréal Group is the world's largest cosmetics company concentrating on hair color products, skin care, sun protection, makeup, perfumes, and hair care. The company is also active in dermatology, toxicology, tissue engineering, and biopharmaceutical research and nanotechnology. Since the 1990s L'Oréal has recruited internationally for its product development teams and has found that the multiculturals in these teams bring a perspective that often leads to unexpected opportunities for product innovation. According to one manager, "Their background is kind of like a master class in holding more than one idea at the same time. They think as if they were French, American, or Chinese all at the same time."[15] For example, a French-Irish-Cambodian team member working in the development of skin care products noticed that many tinted face creams in Asia had a wrinkle reducing, lifting effect. In Europe, these creams tended to be either tinted for use as makeup or lifting for use in skin care. Seeing the opportunity and the increasing popularity of Asian beauty trends in Europe, he and his team developed a tinted cream with lifting effects for the French market that was a huge success.

It stands to reason that the more cultures with which we identify (plurality) the broader the worldview. However, as mentioned in the previous chapter, multiculturals also develop skills that result from reconciling the difference in their multiple cultures. These skills include perceptual acuity, empathy, sensitivity, and, importantly, a more complex way of thinking (*cognitive complexity*). The extent to which these skills are developed depends, in part, on the way in which individuals manage their cultural identity.

Perception is the process by which we interpret the messages we receive from our senses and give meaning to our environment. *Perceptual acuity* is the heighted sense of perception that occurs from perceptual learning. Our cultural conditioning shapes what we pay attention to and what we ignore. For example, in a now classic experiment, Mexican and US children, when presented simultaneously (through a device called a tachioscope) with pictures of a bullfight and a baseball game, perceived the event differently.[16] The Mexican children recalled only the bullfight, while the US children recalled only the baseball game. These two cultural groups had learned to attend to particular stimuli.

Multiculturals, in coming to terms with their various cultural influences, must attend to a wider range of information and through this practice develop a heightened sense of perception. They have had to process this information deeply; therefore, they also develop a heightened *sensitivity* to alternative information. Like Ruth Handler, the creator of the Barbie doll, they see things that those without this perceptual ability do not.

Empathy is the ability to understand the feelings, thoughts, and experiences of another person. Our cultural background has a profound influence on what we think, how we feel, and how we behave; therefore, it is difficult for those outside our culture to be accurate in their understanding of it. When trying to understand culturally different others, we sometimes rely on our stereotype of that culture (e.g., people from the United States will behave in their own self-interest), or we project our own behavior on the situation (e.g., what would cause me to behave that way?).[17] Multiculturals have had to deal with the variety of feelings, thoughts, and experiences associated with their various cultural influences. This experience gives them a heighted sense of empathy. They understand things from the perspective of others.

An important aspect of effectively managing multiple cultural identities is the development of more complex thinking patterns, called *cognitive complexity*. The active and conscious consideration of multiple meaning systems results in changes in the way people organize information in their minds. In fact, the size of the area of the brain devoted to this activity may increase.[18] In order to accommodate the diverse array of values, attitudes, beliefs, and assumptions about appropriate behavior, individuals must find ways to integrate these thoughts and/or create mental linkages between them. They are much less likely to see things as either black or white (right or wrong) and are capable of understanding all the shades of gray in between. Individuals who identify with more than one culture have been found to have more complex thinking patterns than those who identify with a single culture.[19] It is this aspect of multiculturalism that is most directly linked to creativity. That is, it is the experience of effectively managing multiple cultural identities that results in higher levels of cognitive complexity, which in turn is related to more creative solutions.[20]

Thus, the multicultural mind includes a broader worldview,

higher levels of sensitivity and perceptual acuity, greater empathy, and, importantly, more complex ways of thinking. Returning to the example of L'Oréal, a company that has discovered the benefits of nurturing a pool of multicultural managers, we see that multiculturals excel in a certain set of roles:

- They are good at recognizing new product opportunities.

- They serve a role in preventing mistranslation of critical product information.

- They act as cultural translators as well as language interpreters, thereby helping to reduce conflict within teams and with superiors.

- They play an important role in helping teams integrate newcomers who have different sets of behavioral assumptions and modes of communication.

- They help span the boundaries among organizational units situated in different countries.[21]

The way in which L'Oréal takes advantage of the talents of multiculturals may be somewhat specific to the organization and its industry. However, they represent the more general ways in which organizations can leverage this latent talent pool.

Summary

Not every multicultural person understands his or her identity in the same way. Each individual may have a unique way of defining his or her sense of self, but some patterns can be identified based on the number of cultural identities with which a person is concerned (plurality) and the extent to which these identities are integrated. These patterns are *prioritizing, compartmentalizing, hybridizing,* and *aggregating.* The pattern that the person uses depends in part on the way the individual's identity was formed, his or her personal history, and the characteristics of the cultures themselves. The way in which multiculturals make sense of their cultural identities has implications for themselves, for their social relationships, and for how their talents can best be used in organizations. Those individuals who successfully navigate their multiple cultural meaning systems develop a multicultural mind consisting of a broader world view, higher levels of sensitivity and perceptual acuity, greater empathy, and greater cognitive complexity. It is these capabilities that organizations seeking innovation must learn to leverage.

CHAPTER FIVE

SINGING SEA CHANTEYS DOES NOT MAKE YOU A SAILOR

Language and Multiculturalism in an Organizational Context

Individuals who are fluent in more than one language can make a significant contribution to innovation in multicultural organizations. However, multilingual does not mean multicultural any more than singing a seafaring song makes one a sailor.[1] Furthermore, having a multicultural mind does not rely on knowing another language. Language is a powerful element of cultural identity, and second-language ability often forms alongside cultural identity. However, it is important that individuals and organizations do not equate the two. Speaking a *foreign* language is a valuable skill that can give individuals insight into another culture. But language can be just a piece of cultural knowledge, or it can form a key aspect of identity.

Communicating through language involves *codes* (systems of signs that represent a particular idea or concept) and *conventions* (agreed upon norms about how, when, and in what instances these codes will be used). Basically, language is a set of sounds with understood meanings, and the meanings attached to any sound (word) can be completely arbitrary. For example, the Japanese word for cat (*neko*) doesn't look or sound any more like a cat than does the English word. But somewhere in the development of the two languages, these words were chosen to represent the animal, and you just need to know the code. While codes are determined in large part by culture, it is possible to learn them without identifying with their underlying culture. For example, some intercultural communication scholars report that foreign language teachers in the United States are instructed to teach their students foreign languages but to reassure these students that they will not have to change any of their own beliefs in the process.[2] Their values and their sense of identity will not be affected. In this case, language skills consist of knowledge of the codes required to communicate, but without a deep understanding of the culture in which the conventions for language use were formed.

Language Barriers to Innovation

Often the most foreign thing about a foreign culture is the foreign language. Language can be the biggest barrier between people from different cultures. While it's important not to equate multilingualism with a multicultural mind, it's equally important to understand the effects of language in organizations. The act of communication is fundamental to all organizational activities. In particular, and as noted in chapter 1, the most creative idea that is not widely shared and not implemented does not result in innovation. The effective communication of ideas is central to innovation in organizations. Given the changing demographics of organizations, the process of communication must increasingly cross language and cultural barriers. Successful communication requires that the receiver decode and understand the message that is sent. If the sender and the receiver share language and cultural backgrounds, communication is fairly straightforward because both parties know the codes and conventions of language use. Language and cultural differences reduce the amount of common ground the sender and receiver share, thereby making communication more difficult. Even when translators know the codes and the rules for putting them together, sometimes something gets lost in the translation as these notices discovered around the world illustrate:

- In an Austrian ski resort hotel: "Not to perambulate the corridors during the hours of repose in the boots of ascension."

- Outside a Hong Kong tailor shop: "Ladies may have a fit upstairs."

- From a Japanese car rental brochure: "When passenger of foot heave in sight, tootle the horn. Trumpet him melodiously at first, but if he still obstacles your passage then tootle him with vigor."

Cultural conventions affect language, and characteristics of language codes affect cultural conventions. For example, in Cantonese the word for the number four (*sei*) has the same sound as the word for death, whereas the word for the number eight sounds like *faat* (prosperity). As a result, many Chinese people avoid things numbered four and are attracted to the number eight.

To address the problem of communication across languages, many organizations, regardless of their country of origin or where they are based, have adopted English as the common corporate language. For example, in March 2010, Hiroshi Mikitani, the CEO of Japan's largest online retailer, Rakuten, mandated that English would be the official company language, a mandate affecting some 7,100 Japanese employees. More than 550 million people use English on the Internet, and he believed that this new policy would help Rakuten achieve its goal of becoming the number one Internet services company in the world. Its growth had been fueled by mergers and acquisitions in France, Germany, and the United States, and it had established joint ventures throughout Asia. Mikitani demonstrated his seriousness about the change by announcing it to employees in English as opposed to Japanese. By the next day, cafeteria signs, elevator directories, and so on were replaced, and employees were told that they must demonstrate competence in English within two years or risk demotion or dismissal. As of 2012 half of Rakutan's Japanese employees could communicate adequately in English, and 25 percent were doing business in English on a regular basis.[3]

English is spoken by about one-quarter of the world's population, and the competitive pressures of globalization, as well as mergers and acquisitions, have demanded a common language.[4] The second language in use in business is most often English. Although English may have become the lingua franca of business, culture creates differences, even among English speakers. For example, British people live in *flats* and might stand in a *queue* for the *loo,* Americans live in *apartments* and stand in *line* for the *bathroom,* and Canadians live in *suites* and stand in a *lineup* for the *washroom.*

The move toward English as a corporate language is intended to create a mutually accessible language to unite a workforce whose members speak different languages. This replaces the naturally occurring multilingualism that might seem to be unworkable except for limited interactions. Proponents of this approach say that it improves coordination, integration, and organizational learning, as well as shaping the corporate image and giving organizational members a sense of belonging.[5] However, mandating English as the corporate language can have a number of unintended consequences. Second language use requires much more effort on the part of the second language user, which takes attention away from the task at hand. Over long periods of time, second language use is exhausting. So the performance of non-native English speakers can be negatively affected. Also, non-native English speaking employees often feel that they have lost status in the organization and it seems that those with moderate fluency in English are most affected.[6] Those with high levels of fluency can hold their own, while those with low levels feel less pressure to conform. This feeling of loss in status results in resentment and distrust of native English speakers, more comfort with non-native speakers, performance anxiety, and job advancement concerns. For example, the following are reactions to an English-only language policy in a French company:

> The most difficult thing is to admit that one's value as a second-language English speaker overshadows one's real value. In other words, we haven't had the chance to develop our foreign languages for the last 30 years because the company did not ask us to or offer us the opportunity to do so. Now, it is difficult to accept the fact that we are disqualified.

> I'm not really happy with English people thinking that we don't need any other languages, that English is the most shared language . . . and they believe "we can go anywhere and we can do better than you because at least we are native speakers." It's annoying.

I knew that I was an expert, I knew what I was talking about, and I knew that I was right about it. I was proud of my opinions, so I accepted that the language [English] was a little bit frustrating because I wasn't as sophisticated as I would be in my native language. . . . This rule now limits things because I'll perhaps be evaluated on how I talk.

What's going to happen to my career if I don't master the English that's considered to be so important that executives are imposing it in meetings? What's my future?

When we have a conference call to make decisions, or even just when my input is needed, . . . if I'm uncomfortable, my first solution is not to attend the meetings with English coworkers.[7]

These types of reactions may be the reason that research shows that a common corporate language is an ideal often not widely shared by organizational members regardless of corporate attempts to make the company monolingual.[8] The use of a common language may solve many translation issues, but it introduces issues associated with second language use. It is important to innovation for companies to recognize that employees who have key competencies or knowledge but who don't speak the corporate language well may never bring their ideas forward.[9] We have long known that engaging individuals from different cultures generates more ideas. However, these individuals will be reluctant to share their ideas if they feel they will not be understood.[10]

Native speakers of English may also be at a disadvantage in communicating across cultures because their language use is embedded in the conventions of their culture, where for non-native speakers it is not.[11] There are many culturally based barriers to effective communication that have to do with the *conventions* of language use, and not the language being spoken. Two important conventions are communication style and non-verbal behavior.

Cultural norms influence the extent to which language itself is used to communicate a message. The norm in the United States is for people to say exactly what they mean—you just tell it like it is! In contrast, in some other cultures (in the Middle East and Asia, for example) to be polite or avoid embarrassment, communication is much more indirect and implicit. In direct communication, most of the message is in the words being said. In indirect communication, the context—who is speaking, the physical setting, and previous relationships between the parties—are more important. The following examples show a variety of ways to say "no" politely and indirectly.

Saying "No" in Response to "Has my proposal been accepted?"

Conditional "yes"	If everything proceeds as planned, the proposal will be approved.
	Have you submitted a copy of your proposal to the ministry of . . . ?
Criticizing the question	Your question is very difficult to answer.
Refusing the question	We cannot answer this question at this time.
Tangential reply	Will you be staying longer than you had originally planned?
Yes, but	Yes, approval looks likely, but . . .
Delayed answer	You should know shortly.[12]

Effective communication in this case is not a matter of interpreting the *code* but of understanding the *convention* of language use.

Most of us know that we communicate a great deal in nonverbal ways such as body language, gestures, facial expressions, eye contact, tone of voice, and so on. While some people claim to be able to "read others like a book," this is probably only true in a very limited way. The glum facial expression, slumped posture, and lack of eye contact from an athlete who has just lost a match make it unnecessary to ask about the outcome. However, most nonverbal behavior is determined by cultural conventions that make it difficult or impossible for individuals outside that culture to understand it. For example, smiling generally expresses positive feelings. But Asians often smile to conceal nervousness or embarrassment. You may have noticed the giggling-behind-the-hand behavior of some young Asian women when they are embarrassed. While natural facial expressions such as smiling provide a code to understanding others, the conventions for showing emotions (or not) through use of facial expressions can be misleading. As a result, westerners often describe Chinese and Japanese people as inscrutable.

Who can touch whom and on what part of the body is culturally specific. A pat on the back in a low-touch culture (North America, Northern Europe, and Asia) would be meaningful, while in high-touch cultures (Latin America, Southern and Eastern Europe, and the Middle East) it might not even be noticed. And the unspoken message contained in how deeply one Japanese person bows to another in Japan is subtle and complex and nearly impossible for non–Japanese people to master. We often accompany what we are saying with hand and arm movements to reinforce the message, or sometimes gestures are the entire conversation. In both cases, gestures have meanings established by *conventions* in different cultures. The thumb to forefinger with the remaining fingers extended means "okay" all over Latin America except in Brazil, where it is really quite rude. The Hook 'em Horns salute (first and little finger extended with middle fingers held under the thumb) that George W. Bush gave to the University of Texas Longhorns marching band during his inauguration parade was interpreted in Norway as a salute to Satan.[13] The meanings of gestures are governed by cultural conventions and require an understanding of the culture to decode properly.

The implementation of creative ideas to create innovation in organizations requires effective organizational communication. Problems come not only from the use of foreign languages in multicultural organizations but also from the cultural conventions about language use. Enforcing a single corporate language is not the only way to achieve the effective organizational communication that is required for innovation. Furthermore, it may not be the best way to create the kind of open information exchange needed for innovation. Multicultural individuals provide at least part of the answer. Fluency in two or more languages carries with it benefits that can be valuable to organizations managing a workforce composed of multicultural individuals.

Leveraging the Multilingual Multicultural Mind

In addition to being a source of creative ideas, multicultural individuals can solve many of the problems of cross-cultural communication. In the case of L'Oréal mentioned in the previous chapter, one of the roles played by a multicultural was in preventing the mistranslation of critical design features of a new product. An instance in which a product test failed, because of misinterpretation of the specifications of a French manager's product by a German colleague, caused L'Oréal headquarters to recognize the value of multiculturals.[14] The mistranslation was nuanced in that the words were the same, but their meaning was not. It took an English–French–German multicultural to spot the gap in translation.[15]

Multiculturals have internalized the underlying meanings of their multiple cultures; therefore, they are better able to catch differences in the subtle *conventions* of language use as well as in their *codes*. A German (*direct* communication convention) manager talking about his experiences in a Japanese (*indirect* communication convention) subsidiary of a pharmaceutical company put it this way:

> Well, my former boss in Japan was also German. He gave clear instructions to the Japanese. So he thought all was agreed upon. But in fact the Japanese did just the opposite. After one or two of these experiences, you try to switch to Japanese to make sure all is understood well. Maybe, English was too straight . . . or my English was too ambiguous.

A Japanese manager in the same firm commented,

> Usually not many people on the Japanese side are fluent in English. So, I try to put bilingual consultants in between (in order) not to make a barrier. So, I give a freedom to say anything. Raise your hand, if you start to speak Japanese somebody will automatically translate to the rest of the people. So language has not become a problem in our project team.[16]

Using multiculturals as intermediaries, or so-called language nodes, is a strategy that a number of multinational firms have embraced in an effort to improve organizational communication in their culturally diverse environments. It makes sense for several reasons; in addition to the ability to translate not only the code but also the conventions of another language, multicultural employees understand the organizational context and the jargon of the organization. Machine translations or even translations by professional interpreters can't do that. When communication is through electronic media such as e-mail, the context is stripped away entirely, making accurate translation even more difficult.

Jargon, the specialized technical language associated with an organization or group, can be an efficient way to communicate. However, such jargon is almost unintelligible for non–group members. Unless you are a medical practitioner (or have watched too many medical dramas on TV) you probably don't know what a "chem 7" or a "45 c patient" is or what "beating off angels" means. It takes an insider to decode it; literal translations just won't do.

The value of having someone with the ability to translate both the codes and conventions of another language is demonstrated in the following comments from managers in the Russian subsidiary of a Finnish multinational organization:

> We have been lucky enough to have a key person here [Ms. N. N.], who has really been important. She has not only been an interpreter, she has been helping people in the Russian unit in many ways. . . . She has really been much more important than people realize.

> One other person who really knows what is going on there [in the Russian unit] is our assistant [Ms. N. N.]. She has been with [a key Finnish manager] for a very long time and people love her and of course she speaks very fluent Russian and people really trust her, very much so. [The Finnish manager] does

not speak Russian so he is very dependent on her, when he goes there it's the three of them, [the managing director of the Russian subsidiary], Ms. N. N. and [the Finnish manager] and she is "the glue" between them. I would say that she is probably the person in Russia who knows the whole company best.[17]

With their higher levels of sensitivity, perceptual acuity, and empathy, multiculturals are better able to integrate a variety of views, even those that have been presented in other than the dominant language. This reduces the strain of second language use for these individuals and allows them to focus on the task at hand—generating creative ideas! Forcing organization members to communicate only in English, which seems to be a trend,[18] can reduce communication to the level of the least fluent individuals. While there may be certain situations (public events and so on) in which a single corporate language is an advantage, it is unlikely to have a positive influence on innovation.

Summary

While it is important not to equate the ability to speak more than one language with multiculturalism, learning another language often happens alongside the development of multiple cultural identities. Speaking more than one language is a valuable asset in and of itself, but combined with a multicultural mind, it can be a critical source of advantage in fostering the organizational communication required for innovation. Language can be the biggest barrier between people from different cultures and an important indicator of status. Organizations seeking innovation need to generate new ideas, but they also need to implement them. In many organizations, this requires communication across languages and cultures. Some organizations have tried to solve this problem by introducing a single corporate language— very often English. While this approach has some benefits, it has just as many problems, such as creating a status hierarchy based on language fluency and discouraging participation from non-fluent employees, who may have key competencies or knowledge. Requiring English as the corporate language doesn't make individuals better organization members any more than teaching a person a seafaring song makes them a sailor.

Language involves a system of signs that represent ideas called *codes* and also norms about how, when, and in what circumstances codes will be used—called *conventions*. Multilingual multiculturals are capable of understanding both the codes and the conventions of language, including elements such as communication style and nonverbal behavior. Therefore, they are often able to detect subtle differences in meaning that others with only language skills may miss. Multiculturals are often effective as intermediaries or language nodes in the organizational communication system. In addition, the presence of these language nodes allows organization members to contribute in their native language, thus eliminating the negative issues and stress of second language use. Using multiculturals in this way is a strategy that organizations with culturally and linguistically diverse workforces may find useful as they seek to generate and implement new ideas to create innovation. Multilingual multiculturals can contribute by acting as language nodes. However, combined with other skills, they have the capability of taking on many other roles critical to organizational innovation.

CHAPTER SIX

WHERE ARE YOU FROM—REALLY?

Observable Differences and Developing a Multicultural Mind

Where are you from? seems like a simple question. And, for many people with physical characteristics that are typical of a particular geography, it is! But multiculturals often have racial or ethnic backgrounds that don't match their cultural identity.[1] They look "different," and this confuses people. They are difficult to categorize! The following comments from people of mixed race are typical:

> Keko, a mixed race student, had grown weary of her middle school classmates asking her how much Japanese ancestry she had. So when asked, she had systematically responded, "one-third." It amused her that her less mathematically sophisticated classmates often accepted this answer without question. Rarely did they pick up on the fact that you can be one-half Japanese or one-fourth, but not one-third.[2]

> Chela, with Scottish, Jamaican, and East Indian heritage, says, "Being biracial isn't hard because we are confused about our

racial identity. It's hard because everyone else is confused. The problem isn't us—it's everyone else."[3]

Stefanie, an American with German and Chinese ancestry, says, "I hate the obsession people have with what they see as different or exotic. It's so superficial. It gets to me, and I wonder if other mixed people feel that way. I mean, you like the attention yet you don't. It's just another reminder that I'm not like them. . . . When I was younger I thought it was so cool when people called me 'exotic.' But now I really hate that. It's totally demeaning."[4]

Kaylin, a mixed raced student, writes, "Let me explain. I am not white, or in more truthful terms, I am not fully white. I am mixed. My dad was born in Nigeria, while my mother spent the first couple of years of her life in Nova Scotia. Being of any mixed race comes with annoyances. I have lost count of times people have asked me what I am. I suppress the urge to reply, 'I'm human, I think of the female variety, unless I've been mistaken all these years.' And I still have to respond to the typecasting created by my darkened skin. I once had a friend ask me why I didn't act more black. As though having darker skin meant I was predestined to behave in a certain way. I am not black, nor am I white. I am Canadian! People who are half European and half Canadian are never asked the question, 'What are you?' So why in a culture where racial discrimination is so minimal do visible minorities get asked this question? Why is being Canadian not enough of an explanation?"[5]

We live in a complex world. Our surroundings send us much more information than our brains can process.[6] In order to cope with all this information, we have learned to simplify our world by chunking information into a manageable number of categories. The human mind has developed in a way that helps us organize and process information more efficiently. In our minds are structures consisting of categories (called schemas) that develop slowly over time through repeated experiences with objects, people, and situations. These categories are like the pigeonholes into which mail in a non-automated post office is sorted. Each hole might be labeled with the last three digits of a postal code. As letters are sorted, the postal worker does not have to read the name or street address on the letter or even look at the city of the address. The sorter need only glance at the last three digits of the code, and the letter can be sorted into the appropriate pigeonhole. The information processing demands on the sorter are greatly reduced, and the letters can be sorted more quickly.[7]

We have these categories or schemas for a wide variety of things. For example, *fish* describes a category that contains *salmon* but does not perfectly describe a salmon, just as the last three digits of the postal code do not perfectly describe the address of the recipient of a letter. Once we form a category, we use it to understand information that we receive in the future. For example, our knowledge of the category *fish* is used to understand all kinds of fish (swims, has gills, fins, scales, etc.). While useful, this broad category does not distinguish between a salmon and a halibut or any other kind of fish. Our experience influences how elaborate the category is. To people in a fishing community, the idea of a "fish" will be associated with a complex set of mental pictures of different kinds of fish and fishing situations, while the city dweller may see only the fillet that appeared on his/her dinner plate last evening.

In managing organizations we categorize people in the same

way. We think of June as a secretary, Bob as a software engineer, Yuan as Chinese, or Amir as Persian. While categorizing people in this way is a normal part of how our brains deal with information overload, it has numerous consequences, not all of which are good. Yuan may look Chinese, which causes our brains to automatically put her in that category. But having Chinese physical characteristics may have little if anything to do with who Yuan is—her self-concept. It is important that we understand the tendency that we all have to categorize based on observable differences. A number of factors influence this process:

- First, race and gender seem to be universal indicators of a category.

- Second, the extent to which a category stands out has an influence. For example, Anglo-Europeans are obvious in rural Japan.

- Third, the extent to which a person has characteristics that are typical of the group influences categorization. An atypical person such as a brown-haired, dark-skinned Scandinavian would be more difficult for our brains to deal with.

- Fourth, deviations from normal speech in terms of accent, syntax, or grammar influence categorization. A southern US accent is unmistakable to native English speakers and results in immediate categorization.

- Finally, a history of interactions with another group makes it easier for us to categorize them. Our attention is heightened with groups with which we have had a history of conflict.[8]

Stereotypes

Categorizing people influences our attitudes and expectations of them. These stereotypes are based on the limited information we have about a category, as Eric Liu's story shows:

> In the 1980s, when Asian Americans became the country's favorite non-white folk—the "model minority"—Mike Wallace of *60 Minutes* asked: "Why are Asian Americans doing so exceptionally well in school? They must be doing something right. Let's bottle it," . . . the so-called Asian Way.
>
> The Asian Way holds that Asians, unlike non-Asians, prefer order to freedom; that Asians can suffer hardship better than non-Asians; that Asians are more disciplined and virtuous than non-Asians. All of which explains why Asians the world over seem to be doing so exceptionally well.[9]

We can hold intense stereotypes about another culture without any experience with people from that culture.[10] For example, we may expect Americans to be loud and Japanese to be polite without ever having met an American or a Japanese person. There is even a sort of hierarchy of national stereotypes in which some national cultures have higher status because of economic dominance or other desirable characteristics. For example, nationals of less developed countries are often held in lower esteem than people from developed countries such as the United States or Canada.[11] The problem is that once we form a stereotype about a group of people, we apply the stereotype to the same degree to each individual in the category. We expect *all* Japanese to be polite and *all* Americans to be loud. And we will hold on to this expectation in spite of new and contradictory information. To continue with the Japanese example, we might expect Japanese business people to be formal. But when confronted with a Japanese businessperson who exhibits Western informal behavior, we discount that individual as being not typical and maintain our stereotype of Japanese as formal. Cultural stereotypes often overlap with gender, as the appropriate roles for women and men to play in societies vary. Amiee Chan's experience highlights this. With 15 years' experience in executive management and R&D, Amiee Chan (president and CEO of the satellite communications company Norsat) brings a rare blend of technical and corporate strength to her job. Her strategic vision has resulted in consistent revenue growth during her tenure. In commenting on being named one of Canada's 100 most powerful women (for the third time), she said, "I've experienced culturally embedded micro-inequalities as a female leader. On a business trip to Korea, I travelled with a male colleague and everyone assumed he was the CEO and I was his executive assistant. On another occasion, a business partner asked if my father owned Norsat. These situations are frustrating, but it helps to understand that, most of the time, this comes from a lack of awareness."[12]

Stereotypes have another effect that organizations need to be aware of. Since they are based on limited information about members of another culture, they result in less accurate evaluations of that culture. New information about a group for which we hold only a stereotype is evaluated more extremely (more negatively if negative and more positively if positive). The richer our understanding of other cultural groups, the more accurate we are in our evaluations. Because multiculturals have a rich and complex understanding of both or all of their cultures, their ability to detect, process, and organize information about those groups is enhanced.[13] In one of the earliest studies to test the effect of stereotypic expectations on evaluations, Patricia

Linville and Edward Jones conducted a series of experiments based on the assumption that people have less stereotypic (more complex) mental pictures of their own group than they do of other groups.[14] In the first experiment, male and female white participants reviewed a booklet of information on three law school applicants that contained incidental information about the applicants' race and gender, one of whom was black. The applicants' qualifications were good but not outstanding for an applicant to a prestigious law school and, other than race and gender, were identical. The black applicant was judged *more* favorably by white evaluators than an otherwise identical white applicant. In a second experiment, applicants with weak credentials were presented. In this case the black applicant was judged *less* favorably by the white evaluators. Additional experiments confirmed the effect that members of one's own group were judged less extremely.

The lesson from this research is that stereotypes have more of an effect than just reflecting prejudice against others who are not like us. Negative attitudes and prejudicial behavior toward others who look different are of course a source of serious concern. But the natural categorization of people that happens as a result of our limited mental capacity creates a potential minefield of less apparent issues in managing people who look different. The biased evaluations in the previous example are just one of these hidden issues. Another is thinking about our own behavior when trying to understand the behavior of others. That is, when we see others behave in a particular way, we ask ourselves what would cause *us* to behave that way. The danger in this type of thinking is that the culturally based causes for another person's behavior could be very different from our own.

Stereotypes arise from the natural mental categorization that we all do; therefore, we all have them whether we recognize it or not. Anyone who claims not to is just kidding themselves. Failing to address the stereotypic expectations of individuals, particularly if they are supported by the organizational context, can sabotage efforts to leverage the unique skills and abilities of multiculturals.

Monoculturals and a Multicultural Mind

One of the key ways to overcome the negative issues associated with stereotypes is to help monoculturals think more like multiculturals. To do that requires monoculturals to model their development on the experience that leads to a multicultural mind. It is not possible to precisely duplicate the informal experiences of multiculturals that result in a multicultural mind. However, a range of formal methods are available that have been effective in improving the ability of individuals to function in foreign contexts and with culturally different others. The most rigorous of these methods attempts to approximate the multicultural experience. A useful categorization of methods based on social learning theory (the idea that learning is a mental process that involves observing the behavior and attitudes of others, and the outcomes of those behaviors)[15] is shown in figure 6.1.

As shown in the figure, *factual* training involves books, lectures, and briefings about people from a specific background. Learners are passive receptacles for information. *Analytical* training such as case studies or language training requires more active engagement. *Experiential* training such as role plays or simulations involves the highest level of mental involvement. All of these methods can be effective in learning about other people who are different, but, all things being equal, the most effective

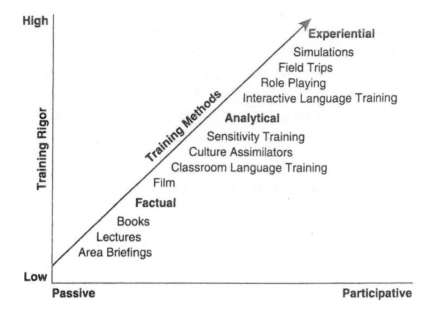

Figure 6.1

Training the multicultural mind

(adapted from Black & Mendenhall, 1989)

methods of developing a multicultural mind are the ones with the most rigor. These methods require the evaluation and reconciliation of differences in values, attitudes, and assumptions about appropriate behavior that leads to a multicultural mind. As discussed in chapter 9, organizations that rely on less rigorous methods to address cultural diversity issues are missing the opportunity to change the way monoculturals think. The obligatory lecture on "valuing diversity" that is prevalent in so many organizations has little if any effect. While formal training has its role in managing diversity, other more experiential avenues may hold more promise.

Part of the answer to reducing the reliance on stereotypic

expectations in today's multicultural organizations exists within the organizations themselves. The opportunity for contact with others who are culturally different is itself part of the solution to the problem. We have long known that appropriate contact between groups with different identities could have a positive effect, as in the following example:

> This is a story of 22 normal 12-year-olds who went to camp one summer at Robbers Cave State Park and became part of an experiment by researchers from the University of Oklahoma. The boys were carefully matched for individual characteristics and divided into two groups who were initially kept separate from each other. The groups spontaneously took on identities, one naming itself the "Rattlers" and the other the "Eagles," and made group flags and so on. As each group became distantly aware of the other, its group identity was reinforced, and it became increasingly territorial about camp facilities. A series of competitive events between the groups was arranged. When the two competing groups were brought together for the first time in the dining hall, there was considerable name calling and singing of derogatory songs, and the groups refused to eat with each another. The conflict continued to escalate and included showing disrespect for each other's flags and raiding of each other's cabins, and some confrontations almost came to blows. Interventions, such as a series of informal get-to-know-each-other events had no effect. Then one day the water supply, which came from a reservoir in the mountains north of the camp, failed, which created a serious problem for everyone. Camp staff blamed vandals, but this was part of the experiment. Finding the source of the water supply problem and ultimately repairing it required the efforts and resources of both the Rattlers and the Eagles. When the water finally began running again, there was

common rejoicing. Over the next few weeks, other challenges were effectively dealt with through the joint efforts of the two groups. On the last day of camp, the campers agreed that it would be a good thing to return home on the bus together.[16]

In this now classic experiment, the joint pursuit of what are called superordinate goals and the sharing of their achievement resulted in a lessening of tensions between the two groups that had developed separate identities. The lessons from Robbers Cave are even more important today than they were 60 years ago when these experiments were conducted. The Rattlers and Eagles of Robbers Cave are replaced in our organizations by numerous groups who are categorized as *different* by members of other groups. And just as at Robbers Cave, casual interventions that involve only superficial engagement by the different groups are unlikely to have an effect. In fact, casual contact of this sort can serve to reinforce stereotypes and strengthen adverse associations. What is required is what has come to be called the *optimal contact strategy*.[17] Positive effects of contact between dissimilar groups occur only in situations having four key characteristics:

- First, it is important that both groups accept and perceive that they have *equal status* within the situation (even though status elsewhere may differ).

- Second, the positive effects of contact require an active, goal-oriented effort, as in repairing the water tank at Robbers Cave.

- Third, the attainment of the common goal must require interdependent effort without intergroup competition.

- Finally, the support of authorities establishes a norm for acceptance of the intergroup contact.

The process that occurs during this type of contact mirrors the development of the multicultural mind outlined in chapter 3.[18] At the initial contact, individuals gain knowledge about the individual who is different and learn that their categorization of him or her may be wrong or at least incomplete (*decategorization*). As they interact over time, they learn not to generalize about members of this cultural group, and they learn to understand and treat them as individuals (*individuation*). Engagement with culturally different others in pursuit of a common goal leads them to understand the value that different perspectives bring to the situation (*appreciation*). Finally, over time individuals integrate these alternative perceptions into their own thinking (*integration*). By recognizing and learning to value differences (by seeing how they can contribute to achieving goals), individuals confront and reconcile differences in their own mind. By integrating alternative perspectives into their thinking, they begin to think like multiculturals. A diagram of this process is shown in figure 6.2.

As indicated in the diagram, differences both in individuals and in the societal and institutional context shape the nature of contact. This general approach should not be expected to work equally well with individuals of all cultures and in all societies and institutions. Previous attitudes and experiences influence whether or not people will engage in contact with culturally different others. Even if this initial resistance is overcome, the results may be less than optimal. For example, research has shown this to be the case with Israeli Arabs and Jews, and with blacks and whites in the United States.[19] However, both societal and institutional characteristics can have a positive influence because all contact is embedded within them. Societal norms for discrimination can make the requirement for equal status within

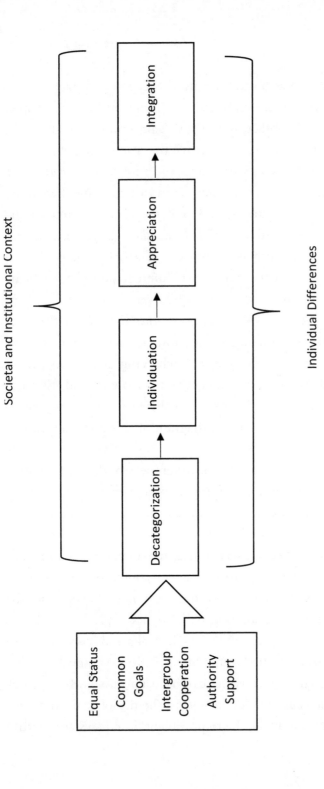

Figure 6.2

Optimal contact and developing a multicultural mind

the situation more difficult to attain, while egalitarian norms make it easier.

As discussed in chapter 9, organizations have the ability to create an environment that produces the characteristics that support *optimal contact*. By doing so they can overcome the myriad issues associated with categorization based on observable characteristics and create not only an environment in which multiculturals can thrive but also one in which monoculturals can develop a multicultural mind.

Summary

Our world is a complex place that presents us with a huge variety in the way people look, talk, and behave. Multiculturals often look "different" because of their mixed backgrounds. They often don't fit a category that conforms to their observable characteristics. This categorization of others is a natural process that results from our brains being incapable of processing the volume and complexity of information that the environment presents to us. The human mind has developed this categorizing process to deal with information more efficiently. Categorizing people in this way is normal, but it has numerous consequences, some of which can be detrimental to effectively leveraging the skills and abilities of multiculturals. The categorizations or stereotypes that result from this process are based on limited information and once formed are applied to every member of the category. They influence our attitudes and expectations of everyone who matches the stereotype. Stereotypes result not only in prejudicial behavior toward others who don't look like us but also in the creation of a number of other issues such as biased evaluations and inaccurate attributions of the behavior of others. Everyone uses these categorizations, so it is important to understand how to overcome the negative effects. One of the important ways of dealing with this issue is to help monoculturals develop a multicultural mind. Part of the solution to this issue exists within multicultural organizations themselves. By employing an optimal contact strategy, organizations can create situations in which different groups have equal status, are engaged in active, goal-oriented activities directed toward the attainment of a common outcome, and are working toward a goal that requires interdependent effort. In this way, monoculturals can progress through the stages of decategorization, individuation, appreciation, and integration and begin to think like multiculturals. Organizations have the ability to create an environment that supports the optimal contact strategy, which makes them a place where the talents of multiculturals can emerge and where monoculturals can develop a multicultural mind.

Part III

LEVERAGING THE MULTICULTURAL MIND

Creating an Innovative Organization

CHAPTER SEVEN

I AM FEELING VERY *OLYMPIC* TODAY, HOW ABOUT YOU?

The Influence of the Situation on Multiculturals and Innovation

Sometimes the importance of the situation is the overriding influence on the behavior of multiculturals and on the creative process. The quotation in the chapter title is from Sanka Coffie (played by Doug E. Doug), the brakeman of the world's first Jamaican bobsled team, depicted in the 1993 movie *Cool Runnings*. Despite having no experience in the Olympics, he was expressing his feelings of an Olympic identity when he and his teammates were qualifying for the Calgary Winter Olympic Games. Sanka's expression suggests the powerful influence that a strong situational context can have on the way people feel, think, and act.

In July 1961 a series of experiments showed just how powerful the situation can be.

> Forty men solicited by direct mail and a newspaper ad were paid to participate in a laboratory experiment at Yale University. Participants were ordered by an administrator (a role played by a 31-year-old high school teacher dressed in a gray lab coat) to

administer an electric shock to a victim (another role, played by a 47-year-old accountant who had been trained to respond systematically) who was bound to an electric chair in another room. The justification for administration of the shock was a cover story about studying the effects of punishment on learning. A simulated generator was used that had 30 marked voltage levels ranging from 15 to 450 volts, with labels ranging from "Slight Shock" to "Danger: Severe Shock." A number of steps were taken to convince the participants of the realism of the situation. The participant was instructed to administer increasingly higher levels of shock each time the victim (learner) gave a wrong answer to a series of questions, even to the point of reaching the level marked "Danger: Severe Shock." As the experiment proceeded, some participants showed resistance and were encouraged by the administrator with "Please continue," "The experiment requires you to continue," "It is absolutely essential that you continue," and finally "You have no choice, you must go on." All 40 participants administered shocks at the 300-volt mark, at which point the victim could be heard to pound the wall of the room in which he was bound to the electric chair. He no longer responded to questions after this time. Five participants refused to go on beyond this point, and four more administered only one more shock. Although obedient participants continued, they often did so under extreme stress. They were observed to sweat, tremble, stutter, bite their lips, groan, and dig their fingernails into their skin. Despite their reluctance 26 of the 40 participants proceeded to punish the victim until they reached the most powerful shock available on the generator![1]

You may recognize the preceding description as Stanley Milgram's classic experiment. It is often taught in psychology courses as a study of obedience to authority, and that is partly what it was about. But, more broadly, it describes the behavior of individuals in response to a strong situation despite their personal beliefs about not harming others. The characteristics of this situation included the presence of an administrator, who by virtue of little more than a lab coat was in a position of authority, as well as an impressive experimental laboratory, the fact that they had been paid to be there, and the participants' remoteness from the victim. It is not the dramatic characteristics of the situation described in the experiment that are important but the more general understanding of the importance of the effect of the situation on behavior and how organizations can influence it.

Flexible Situations and Intrinsic Motivation

All organizations create *situations* that influence the behavior of multiculturals and the creative process in either a positive or negative way. This can occur either formally through the explicit rules and regulations in the organization or informally through the implicit understandings that people have about how they should behave. This informal aspect of the organization or *organizational culture* is important because it can provide a sense of identity for organization members and also a mechanism for socializing organization members into a way of doing things that is consistent with the goals of the organization. We used to think that organizations needed a strong culture in which all employees shared a set of values to be successful.[2] The idea was that this strong culture would substitute for more formal methods of organizing work and directing behavior. We now know that *strong* cultures create *strong* situations that can promote *dysfunctional* behaviors and have *negative* effects. Organizational culture provides organization members with a set of behaviors that may have worked well in the past. However, what organizations seeking innovation want are ideas that will work well in the future. The lesson is that if you want innovation, you need to create *flexible* situations, not strong ones. This may sound counterintuitive, but strong situations constrain opinions and provide clear signals about what is expected, which creates less variation in the behavior of individuals. For example, the requirement for concrete answers (called the need for cognitive closure) creates a strong situation. Research shows that this strong situation reduces the effect of multicultural experience on individuals' receptiveness to ideas from foreign cultures.[3] The skills and abilities of multicultural individuals are more likely to emerge when organizational signals and constraints on behavior are weak. For example, Google is one of the most innovative companies around, and it boasts an informal bottom-up process for new-product development.

Marissa Mayer, Google's former vice president of search products and user experience had this to say:

> Ideas for new product development come from everywhere—
> every employee, every department, from both necessity and
> serendipity. By creating an environment where ideas can be
> freely exercised, like a muscle, they will likely get more toned
> and more in tune with the organization's circulation. We still
> don't do very high-definition product specs. If you write a
> 70-page document that says this is the product you're supposed
> to build, you actually push the creativity out with process. The
> engineer who says, you know what, there's a feature here that
> you forgot that I would really like to add. You don't want to
> push that creativity out of the product. The consensus-driven
> approach where the team works together to build a vision around

what they're building and still leaves enough room for each member of the team to participate creatively, is really inspiring and yields us some of the best outcomes we've had.[4]

Overcontrol in organizations is probably the factor that most impedes creativity. But saying that organizations need to create flexible situations that avoid this kind of overcontrol is only part of the answer to creating conditions that promote creative performance. It is the work environment combined with the creative ability of the multicultural mind that we need to understand. Research has overwhelmingly indicated that an important way in which the work environment influences creativity is through the creation of intrinsically interesting work.[5] People are most creative when they are intrinsically motivated (the desire to work on something for its own sake) rather than extrinsically motivated by surveillance, competition, superiors, or external rewards. In fact, the addition of extrinsic rewards to an already intrinsically interesting task can reduce intrinsic motivation as the following story illustrates:

> The story goes that there was a grumpy old man who lived next door to a vacant lot where youngsters played baseball after school. Because the noise bothered him, the old man hatched a plan. One day he went to the children and told them that he enjoyed watching them play so much that he would pay each of them a quarter for every day that they played there. The children were surprised that anyone would pay to see them play. However, the next day and every day that week the old man gave each child a quarter. The next week, however, he announced that he could no longer afford a quarter and would only be able to pay a dime. While a few of the children expressed their disappointment, they took it in stride, as they had

intended to play in any case. The next week the old man reduced the payment to a nickel, and a few days after that he announced that he had bad news and would no longer be able to pay them anything. On hearing this, the children were angry and said, "If you think we are going to play here for nothing you're crazy!" They left and never returned.[6]

The old man had succeeded in robbing them of the pleasure of playing baseball, thereby decreasing their intrinsic motivation to play next to his house.

When people are interested in engaging in an activity because of the work itself (intrinsically motivated), they are free of outside concerns, likely to take more risks, to explore new ways of doing things, and to be playful with ideas and materials.[7] The question then is how to create work situations that are intrinsically motivating so that the creativity of the multicultural mind can surface.

The Work Situation and Intrinsic Motivation

Two characteristics of the work situation are particularly important to intrinsic motivation. These are the complexity of the job and the style of supervision.

Complex, challenging jobs have the following characteristics:

- *Skill Variety:* The job requires various activities, requiring the worker to develop and use a variety of skills and talents.

- *Task Identity:* The job requires the jobholder to identify and complete a piece of work with a visible outcome.

- *Task Significance:* The job affects other people's lives. The influence can be either in the immediate organization or in the external environment.

* *Autonomy:* The job provides the employee with significant freedom, independence, and discretion to plan out the work and determine the procedures in the job. For jobs with a high level of autonomy, the outcomes of the work depend on the worker's own efforts, initiatives, and decisions rather than on instructions or a manual of job procedures.

* *Feedback:* Individuals are provided with clear, specific, detailed, *actionable* information about the effectiveness of their job performance. When people receive clear, actionable information about their work performance, they have better overall knowledge of the impact of their work activities and what specific actions they need to take (if any) to improve.[8]

When jobs are more complex and challenging, people are more excited about their work and interested in completing tasks in the absence of external controls.

Another part of the work situation related to creative performance is the style of supervision. Supervision can be either *supportive* or *controlling.* Supportive supervision shows concern for employees' feelings and needs, encourages them to voice their own concerns, provides positive informal feedback, and aids in skill development. In contrast, controlling feedback closely monitors employee behavior and generally pressures employees to think, feel, and behave in a particular way. Controlling supervision creates strong situations that undermine intrinsic motivation and reduce creative performance. Research shows that the highest creative performance occurs in individuals who have creative skills (such as multiculturals) when they are working in complex, challenging jobs and are supervised in a supportive, non–controlling fashion.[9]

Organizational Context and Creative Performance

In addition to the complexity and challenge of the job itself and the style of supervision, several other characteristics of the organizational context can influence creative performance by creating flexible situations. Organizations that support risk-taking behavior, have adaptive organizational structures, and support informal information exchange are likely to have higher creative performance. Consistent with the idea of creating flexible situations to foster creativity, organizations that encourage people to take risks and have a tolerance for failure will have higher creativity. As Arianna Huffington said, "We need to accept that we won't always make the right decisions, that we'll screw up royally sometimes—understanding that failure is not the opposite of success, it's part of success."

Encouraging risk taking can be represented in both the organizational culture and in more formal reward systems. Likewise, adaptive organizational structures, as opposed to rigid hierarchies, result in higher creative performance.

The availability of information is a critical aspect of the creative process. Constraints on information flows will create strong situations that have a negative effect on creativity, whereas organizations that support informal information exchange will have higher creative performance. For example,

> in 1944 Joseph Simons approached the 3M Company for
> funding to continue work on a process he had invented to
> make fluorochemicals (little was known about these chemicals
> except that they wouldn't mix with anything except other
> fluorochemicals). Intrigued by these compounds, 3M chairman
> William McKnight and president Richard Carlton bought the

rights to the process. They formed a group in 3M's research laboratory to see what they might make of the fluorochemicals. By 1949 about one-quarter of 3M's research budget was committed to the project, but none of the creative people involved had identified a potential commercial application. About this time the flourochemical research group received a needed boost. The US Air Force contracted with 3M to develop a new flourochemical rubber for use in the hundreds of rubber seals and hoses in jet aircraft; no known rubber could withstand the many hours of exposure to hot jet fuel. Working on this project was JoAn Mullin, a young research chemist. In mid-July 1953 Mullin was pouring a batch of flourochemical-based synthetic latex into a flask. She accidentally spilled three small drops on her brand-new light blue deck shoes. By the end of the day, the spots on her shoes had disappeared, and she forgot about it—until the weekend. Mullin had a habit of soaking her cotton deck shoes in soapy water every Saturday so they would be clean for the following week. However, on this Saturday when she put her shoes in the water, the spots reappeared. The light blue color of her shoes darkened when wet, except for the spots, which remained light because they were dry. On the following Monday, she told her colleagues about what happened. Knowing that other groups were working on oil and water repellent treatments, her supervisor, George Rathman, dipped some swatches of blue jean cloth into the synthetic latex and gave them to Hugh Bryce, who was in charge of the fluorochemical applications group. However, there was little initial interest because researchers had already tried a similar substance and were convinced that it did not work. The fabric swatches were relegated to a desk drawer. Mullin continued to wash her shoes every weekend, and some six months later the spots were still remaining dry. She asked Rathman about the tests on the swatches. Rathman called Bryce with the news of the long-lasting effect, and the tests were finally done by a researcher who was "looking for something interesting to work on." The potential was confirmed, the project became official, and after hundreds of additional tests, two 3M chemists, Patsy Sherman and Samuel Smith, patented the formula that would become Scotchgard.[10]

It is unlikely that the invention of the stain and water repellent Scotchgard would have occurred without the informal communication that occurred before the project became official. The flexible organizational structure and an environment that supported risk taking (typical in many research labs) certainly contributed as well. A rigid formal structure, which created a strong situation, that did not allow for informal information transfer across organizational units would almost certainly have thwarted the process.

The informal collaboration that is important to creativity and innovation can be promoted in a variety of ways, including the physical environment in which employees work. Pixar's Emeryville, California, headquarters is an example. Designed under the guidance of then CEO Steve Jobs, the campus includes an atrium space that acts as a central hub. The atrium houses reception, employee mailboxes, a café, foosball tables, a fitness center, two 40-seat viewing rooms, and a large theater. According to Jobs, "If a building doesn't encourage collaboration, you'll lose a lot of innovation and the magic that's sparked by serendipity. So we designed the building to make people get out of their offices and mingle in the central atrium with people they might not otherwise see."[11]

Diversity Climate and Level of Cultural Diversity

So far, the organizational factors that contribute to a positive situational context for creativity and innovation could be applied to almost any organization and any set of employees. However, there are two conditions that are specific to multicultural individuals. These are the diversity climate and the organization's level of cultural diversity.

The diversity climate of an organization is the degree to which an organization's members promote and value diversity. A number of characteristics of a positive diversity climate have been identified. They fall into four groups:

- Degree of intergroup conflict and acceptance of others (e.g., high intergroup communication, openness of informal networks, low power difference between groups)
- Institutional commitment to diversity (e.g., recruitment, promotions, compensation, physical work environment, employee development across cultural groups)
- Fairness (e.g., pluralism in acculturation, lack of institutional bias)
- Generalized atmosphere of respect (e.g., low identity prejudice, low stereotyping, low ethnocentrism)[12]

Decades of research has shown that a positive diversity climate results in favorable outcomes both for employees and the organization.[13] With regard to the creative performance of multiculturals, a positive diversity climate reduces prejudicial behavior toward others who are different and ensures the fullest possible participation of all organization members. The most creative idea that is not voiced because the individual feels their view will not be understood or valued will not result in innovation.

Also, as discussed in chapter 9, organizations with a visibly positive diversity climate will have greater success in recruiting and retaining individuals with a multicultural mind.

Related to diversity climate is the amount of cultural diversity that exists within the organization. Recent research shows that the ability and motivation of multicultural individuals to engage in the organization is affected by the existing level of cultural diversity. Multicultural individuals in monocultural organizations tend to either suppress or defend the foreign aspect of their identity. For example, an Arab American in a 400-person monocultural American workforce had this to say:

> I did try not to be too Arab. I didn't really voice my opinions on what I felt would be very hot topics, especially if it's related to events in the Middle East like wars. . . . Not that I felt that I couldn't share my opinion, I just felt that then I would have to defend who I am. And I just felt that I didn't want to do that. I didn't want to have to try to defend the fact that I'm Arabic, that I'm of Middle Eastern descent. So I always felt that I had to be way more American for that.

Some organizations have two primary cultural groups represented. In that case, multiculturals feel that they are valued for the different perspectives they bring, but they are also constrained from identifying too much with either of their cultures. For example, a Chinese Canadian teacher in a formerly all-Caucasian school said:

> I sometimes feel like a union steward [representative]. Sometimes probably people hate you because you do something they don't like. You're always struggling between you are useful sometimes, you are useless sometimes, you are hopeless sometimes, you are hopeful. . . . In the past 20 years, they get used to Chinese,

so they don't want to be more Chinese anymore. This is why
you feel resistance in your working place. I want to make a
contribution to this working place. But . . . I think people start
to feel they should resist.

Finally, culturally heterogeneous organizations allow multiculturals to bring both of their identities to the job. For example, a
Chinese Canadian employee had this to say:

> Our organization is really multicultural, and almost one-quarter
> of the employees are immigrants. So . . . you don't have to hide
> from your culture or background. And also I could benefit
> from my bicultural background because, you know, I am always
> volunteering for programs, and lots of volunteers are from Asia
> and from China. And actually I benefit a lot from my bicultural
> background.[14]

It is clear that the diversity climate and the level of cultural
diversity go hand in hand. A positive diversity climate allows all
organization members, regardless of their cultural background or
visible indications of being different, to fully engage in the organization, whereas the level of cultural diversity in the organization helps to accomplish this by promoting meaningful contact
as discussed in chapter 6. Multiculturals who feel comfortable
with both their identities at work (the catchphrase these days is
bringing your whole self to work) are more likely to generate
the kind of novel ideas and solutions required for innovation.
For all organizations, but especially those without high levels
of existing cultural diversity, an important question is how to
attract and retain individuals with a multicultural mind. Organizations must not only signal a positive climate for diversity in
order to attract multiculturals; they have to make this aspect of
their culture a reality in order to retain these valuable resources.

Summary

The importance of the situation in influencing the way people feel, think, and act cannot be overestimated. All organizations create a situational context that can have either a positive or negative influence on the creative behavior of multicultural individuals. Organizations influence the work situation either through formal rules and regulations or informally through the culture of the organization. We used to think that the most effective organizations had strong cultures in which all employees shared an understanding of how to behave. However strong cultures create strong situations that constrain opinions and provide clear signals about what is expected. Organizations that want innovation need to create flexible situations, not strong ones! In these work environments, the creative abilities of individuals are more likely to emerge. An important way in which the work environment influences creativity is through the creation of intrinsically interesting work. People are most creative when they have the desire to work on something for its own sake as opposed to being motivated by external rewards. When people are intrinsically motivated, they take more risks, explore new ways of doing things, and are playful with ideas and materials. Two factors are important in creating intrinsically interesting work situations:

- Designing complex challenging jobs
- Ensuring supportive as opposed to controlling supervision

Additionally, organizations that encourage risk taking, have adaptive, flexible organizational structures, and support informal information exchange will encourage higher creativity and innovation. There are two additional organizational conditions that influence the creative performance of multiculturals. These are the diversity climate of the organization and its level of cultural diversity. In order to gain the active participation of multiculturals, who are often categorized as "different," it is important that they feel that they are capable of fully engaging in the organization and that their views are valued. Organizations need to recognize that they signal the nature of the work environment through their overt statements, organizational policies, and references to their history and reputation. In order to attract and retain multicultural employees, organizations must craft these messages to reflect a positive climate for diversity that is the reality in the organization.

CHAPTER EIGHT

I GET BY WITH A LITTLE HELP FROM MY FRIENDS

The Roles of Multiculturals in Teams and Organizations

Much of the work of organizations is now done in work groups or teams. As knowledge-based competition becomes the norm, the contribution of teams to innovation is even more important to understand. Not only are individuals with multicultural minds a source of creative ideas, they have important and unique roles to play in organizations and teams seeking innovation. Individuals in culturally diverse organizations can be a source of innovation. However, as the line from the Beatles' song in the chapter title suggests, in order to be effective contributors, they may need a little help from their (multicultural) friends.

Culturally diverse teams have the opportunity for superior performance, but that same diversity can be a source of problems, which must be managed.

For example, in a famous case of drunk flying, Japan Airlines cargo flight 8054 carrying the pilot (a 53-year-old US national), two copilots (both Japanese, aged 31 and 35), two cargo handlers, and 65 beef cattle crashed shortly after takeoff in Anchorage,

Alaska, killing all on board. Post-mortem analysis indicated that the captain had a blood alcohol level of .29 percent (a driver in the United States with .08 percent is considered legally intoxicated). The captain's preflight behavior included staggering and slurring his words and was noticed by the driver who took the crew to the airport. The National Transportation Safety Board determined that the probable cause of the accident was "a stall that resulted from the pilot's control inputs aggravated by airframe icing while the pilot was under the influence of alcohol. Contributing to the cause of this accident was the failure of the other flight crew members to prevent the captain from attempting the flight." The cockpit voice recorder showed that neither the first nor the second officer remarked about the captain's intoxication, nor did they try to deter him from controlling the aircraft. Subsequent investigation attributed the reluctance of the junior flight crew members to confront the captain to the fact that suggesting to the captain, their superior, that he delegate the takeoff to a junior crew member would have caused him to lose face.[1]

The failure of the Japanese junior officers to intervene in the case of Japan Airlines flight 8054 may be an extreme example of the influence of culture in a team. However, the expectation that individuals have about their roles is a powerful influence on their behavior in organizations. In this case the Japanese pilots saw themselves as subordinate to the captain, and Japanese norms for behavior with a superior resulted in their reluctance to act. Individuals develop the expectations that they have about their role in the organization from several sources. One of these sources is the messages that the organization sends to prospective employees about the expectations that the organization has of them. Another is how individuals see themselves fitting into the organization or group based on their sense of who they are—their self-identity. Because of having more than one cultural influence on their self-identity, multiculturals are particularly well suited to certain roles in organizations and teams. The organization, because of its powerful influence on the situation, can either foster these roles to take advantage of the multicultural mind or suppress them by creating incompatible imposed roles for these employees. The power of roles to influence individual behavior is dramatically demonstrated in the following example.

> It was 1971, and the basement of the Stanford University Psychology Department had been converted into a mock but realistic prison. Twenty-four male university students were selected for psychological normality and paid $15 a day to participate. Participants were assigned by the flip of a coin to the role of either prisoner or guard in a simulated prison environment. The simulation was kept as realistic as possible. Prisoners were arrested at their own homes, without warning, and taken to the local police station. They were then transported to the mock prison where they were stripped naked, deloused, their possessions were removed, and they were issued prison clothing (a smock and nylon cap and a chain around one ankle), which identified them only by number. They were then locked up. Guards had been issued military-like khaki uniforms, whistles, and handcuffs, and they wore reflecting sunglasses.
>
> The prisoners and guards immediately began settling into their roles even though they had been given no formal instructions about how to behave. Within hours some guards began to harass prisoners, behaving in a brutal and sadistic manner. Other guards followed this lead, and prisoners were tormented, taunted, made to do push-ups, and given pointless

tasks. Prisoners adopted prisoner-like behavior. Over time, they became submissive and obedient. After 36 hours one prisoner began showing signs of serious emotional disturbance and was removed from the experiment. Three other participants also became so distressed that they had to be removed. As the days went on, the relationship between prisoners and guards deteriorated; the guards became more aggressive and assertive, demanding even greater obedience from prisoners. The situation became so powerful that even the experimenter, who was only supposed to be an observer, began to think of himself as a prison warden as opposed to a researcher. Although the simulation had been scheduled to last two weeks, because of fear that it would result in permanent mental or physical harm, it was terminated after six days.[2]

The preceding is a description of one of the most famous experiments in psychology in which normal university students behaved in ways consistent with their randomly assigned roles as opposed to their internalized values and beliefs.[3] It shows how powerful the roles to which people are assigned can be in shaping their behavior. It also shows how easily organizations can create role expectations for their employees, either intentionally or unintentionally. Organizations seeking innovation need to be cautious about creating role expectations, either formally or informally, that do not allow multiculturals to play out their innate roles.

Multicultural Roles in Teams

Individuals who have developed a multicultural mind have a broader worldview, higher levels of sensitivity and perceptual acuity, greater empathy, and more complex ways of thinking.

These skills allow them to function well in a number of organizational and team roles. The higher level of cognitive complexity that has resulted from effectively managing their multiple identities allows multiculturals to be more creative.

However, multiculturals fit naturally into a number of roles important to innovation beyond being the engine for the generation of creative ideas. The roles they play in multicultural teams can have a dramatic effect on team effectiveness.

> When you have a very diverse team—people of different
> backgrounds, different culture, different gender, different age,
> you are going to get a more creative team—probably getting
> better solutions, and enforcing them in a very innovative
> way and with a very limited number of preconceived ideas.
> (Carlos Ghosn, CEO of Renault-Nissan)[4]

Harnessing the creativity of multicultural teams is a key pathway to organizational innovation. We have long known that culturally diverse teams generate more ideas and that they have the potential to reach better solutions to problems than single culture teams.[5] However, the same cultural diversity that leads to more and different ideas also results in culturally different perceptions, expectations, and communication patterns that can have damaging effects on team performance (as we saw in the case of drunk flying). These negative effects (called *process losses*) include the formation of faultlines between culturally different groups, increased performance time, higher levels of conflict, and lower levels of team member participation. The presence of multiculturals in teams can help to reduce these process losses and improve creative performance.[6] Multiculturals improve team creativity by performing the three key roles of *bridges, integrators,* and *mediators.*[7]

Bridges. Individuals bring their culturally based norms for how work groups should function to culturally diverse teams. When the workgroup is composed of a few different cultures (as opposed to many cultures) individuals form subgroups based on culture. Information flow across subgroup boundaries is reduced because the larger group is divided along these so-called fault lines.[8] Multiculturals can bridge this cultural divide because of their cultural knowledge, their ability to relate to members of both cultures, and often their language skills. They can explain the perspectives of the different group members, improve knowledge sharing in the group, reduce the tendency to use redundant information or make premature decisions. Bridging across these intragroup boundaries reduces the time that culturally diverse teams take to reach a conclusion.

Integrators. Culturally different workgroup members are aware that they are different. Based on this awareness, they compare themselves to the other members of the group and evaluate their status in the team and whether their participation will be valued or evaluated negatively. As John Cleese said, "Nothing will stop you from being creative so effectively as the fear of making a mistake." If individuals perceive their status in the group as high, they are likely to participate more fully and to feel more positive about the group. When other group members are perceived as being different, individuals are often reluctant to invest high amounts of effort in interacting because they feel this will cost more in time and effort than the potential benefit. The Japanese flight officers, in the story that opened this chapter, were reluctant to act, in part because of their perceived low status and the feeling that taking over from the captain would be viewed negatively.

High status also conveys to the individual a sense of power to influence others by increasing confidence in his or her thoughts and perspectives. Recent research shows that individuals who feel empowered generate creative ideas that are less influenced by the situation.[9] Creative performance in teams depends on the full exchange of ideas by group members. Multicultural individuals, with their high levels of sensitivity and empathy, encourage the full exchange and integration of ideas by helping all group members feel comfortable with their status in the group and are able to share their ideas and fully participate. The variety of perspectives held by multiculturals helps reduce the tendency for teams to conform to solutions proposed by a dominant group (called *groupthink*).[10] By encouraging the expression of alternative views, they help the team focus on *how* the team is functioning as opposed to a somewhat mindless rush toward solutions.

Mediators. Working together in teams, often under time pressure, produces conflict, but conflict comes in several forms.[11] There is conflict that comes from interpersonal differences, conflict that results from different views regarding the team task, and controversies about how to accomplish the task (process-related conflict). The opportunity for all three types of conflict is greater in culturally diverse teams than in single culture teams. However, not all conflict is bad. High-performing teams tend to have low levels of relationship and process-related conflict, but higher levels of task conflict. Surfacing differences of opinion about the task may result in conflict, but it also produces better solutions. Not only do culturally diverse teams have more conflict, but their members can also have different approaches to solving conflicts.[12] For example, Japanese might like to refer conflicts to a higher authority, Germans might prefer referring to rules and procedures, and Americans may seek to discover the underlying cause of the conflict.[13] When conflicts arise, multiculturals can use their skills to minimize the destructive interpersonal and process-related conflict and bring about an agreement or recon- ciliation. Their ability to see issues from multiple perspectives allows them to understand the often culturally based sources of conflict and to take appropriate action. Their multiple identities allow them to be perceived as neutral and not aligned with any one group, as the following story illustrates.

> Joanne Qiu, born in Hong Kong but raised and educated in Canada (MBA from Simon Fraser University), had recently joined the product development team at Vancouver-based Startech Industries. The team's job was to come up with ways to market Startech's satellite-based technology products to Asia. The team seemed to be stalled, and Joanne's job was to see if she could get them moving. The four other team members have very different cultural backgrounds. Steve, an American is the official team leader. He has strong ideas about what the product offering should look like; he talks about it a lot, and tries to persuade his colleagues. Ulrike, a recent immigrant from Germany, has ideas about products that are not only different from Steve's but diametrically opposed. And, she has 20 years of experience in the industry in Germany. She is not about to back down from her ideas and thinks that she has forgotten more about satellite technology than Steve has ever known. She too speaks loudly and forcefully about the offering. Steve doesn't agree with her and argues back just as loudly.
>
> The other members of the team keep a low profile. Juan, a technical expert from Mexico, can't stand Ulrike. How does she dare talk to the team leader like that? She has no respect for authority! It's not so much that Juan doesn't agree with Ulrike's

ideas—in fact he secretly thinks they are good—it's just the rude and aggressive way she presents them that he objects to. She acts as if she were Steve's equal if not above him. Juan would not support Ulrike's ideas if his life depended on it. Yuan from Taiwan is the final member of the group. Her knowledge of the Asian market is an important element in the decision. However, she doesn't feel that Steve really wants her opinions and ideas. He says he wants to hear from everyone, but she doesn't think he means it. If he does, why does he argue so aggressively with Ulrike? Yuan thinks if you really want to hear what other people think you should show them respect. Listening to Steve and Ulrike makes Yuan sad. These people are talented but completely egocentric. She puts forth her views when the opportunity arises, but so timidly that Steve wonders if Yuan herself believes what she is saying.

It didn't take Joanne long to understand what was happening in the team she had just joined. Everyone had good ideas, but the conflict between individuals was preventing them from being understood and discussed effectively. Even though she wasn't the team leader, she used her newness to the group as an opportunity to make a suggestion. She said, "You all seem to know each other's views well. But, so I can get a better understanding of where we are I wonder if I can make a suggestion. Can each of us write down our ideas on a card? Then we will shuffle the cards, deal them out, and each read an idea in turn. That way we separate the idea itself from the person presenting it." By this time the group was so frustrated that they agreed. And it didn't take long before agreement on a marketing strategy was reached.[14]

In the preceding story, multicultural Joanne did not have deep knowledge of the cultures of any of the other team members. The role she took in helping the team to achieve its goal was to *facilitate* the interactions of the parties. If she had deep knowledge of the other cultures, research shows that she would have been more likely to intervene more directly to resolve the issues.[15]

Virtual Teams. Not all teams interact face to face. One way in which organizations are dealing with the challenges of globalization is by forming work groups with geographically dispersed structures. These *virtual teams* interact primarily by electronic networks. The advantage of virtual teams is the ability to choose group members regardless of geographic boundaries. However, virtual teams have special challenges in *communicating, relationship building and conflict management,* and *task management.*[16] The skills that multiculturals bring to these teams can help resolve these issues. Communication in virtual teams relies on electronic media and most often the written word, such as e-mail. Because the language used is usually English, this may help second language speakers who are conversationally weak. However e-mail is not a very rich communication medium, and it can mask cultural differences. A straight-to-the-point e-mail from a person from a direct-communication culture can easily be misinterpreted by a colleague from an indirect-communication culture who needs information about the context to understand. The multicultural mind is able to catch these subtle differences and improve communication in virtual teams.

Virtual teams often have less conflict because they interact though electronic media. However, this means they lose the physical contact that helps develop trust, respect, cooperation, and commitment that a cohesive team needs to function effectively. Because the multicultural mind understands the context of the various cultures involved, multiculturals can be the glue that holds these far-flung work groups together.

Different tasks require different team processes and strategies. The exchange of the tacit knowledge (in-the-bones knowledge as opposed to more explicit easy-to-record ideas) required to generate creative solutions proposes an additional challenge for virtual teams. In face-to-face teams, individual roles and clear task strategies and norms for interaction can be resolved on a continuous basis. Virtual teams have little opportunity to manage the task process in this way. Multiculturals can use their skills to act as a coordinating mechanism in which they encourage participation that allows the knowledge of group members to be leveraged, helps to foster a strong group identity, and creates an environment of trust. While virtual teams face additional barriers to creative performance, the advantage of being able to select team members without geographic restrictions can result in teams than are even more creative than face-to-face teams—if the challenges are appropriately managed.

Multiculturals as Boundary Spanners in Organizations

Of course, teams do not exist in a vacuum. They operate inside the organization in which they are embedded, and the characteristics of the organization can influence the creative performance of teams. The strategy of the organization, the authority structures, and the regulations employed to implement that strategy determine which groups in organizations get resources and which behaviors get rewarded. Large, profitable organizations can provide more resources for any type of group. However, just throwing resources at multicultural teams may not be the best solution. In some cases, teams generate greater innovation by making do with what is at hand.[17] What is more important is making sure that teams have the skills and attitudes to perform well. It's also important to remember that team members must first be organization members, so the selection process of the organization will determine the individuals available to form teams. As Steve Jobs said, "Innovation has nothing to do with how many R&D dollars you have. When Apple came up with the Mac, IBM was spending 100 times more on R&D. It's not about money. It's about the people you have, how you're led, and how much you get it."

Multiculturals can draw on their skills to engage in activities across the organization that can have a positive influence on innovation. These activities can include mediating, brokering, or negotiating between different organizational groups (sometimes in different countries), acting as language nodes to improve organizational communication, facilitating the integration of newcomers, helping to develop monoculturals, and leading organizations in the management of diversity. A key element in all of these activities is that they involve spanning a boundary of some sort. Boundary spanning involves four general tasks that multiculturals can perform in the organization.[18] These are *exchanging, linking, facilitating,* and *intervening.*

Exchanging of information happens when multiculturals transmit information and knowledge across organizational boundaries. This can take place in formal meetings, horizontal arrangements such as task forces, or informal networks.

Linking is the use of personal networks to enable previously disconnected organization members to link up across boundaries. Multiculturals often have personal networks that cross cultural and organizational boundaries.

Facilitating is assisting in the cross-boundary interactions of others, for example by acting as the channel through which messages are delivered.

Intervening is the active participation in resolving misunderstandings and building intergroup trust.

By engaging in these activities across cultural contexts, multiculturals develop a loose and varied social network that improves the free exchange of information that is critical to organizational innovation. All multiculturals are not the same. Because multiculturals manage or experience their multiple identities in different ways, they may be more effective in some of these roles than in others. It may be tempting to try to identify multicultural types and match them logically to appropriate roles. However, in reality, it's very difficult to understand how multiculturals are dealing with their identities except by observing their behavior. Organizations should therefore try to attract a wide range of multiculturals and create an environment that allows their skills to emerge and allows them to migrate to roles in which they feel comfortable. Once more is known about them as individuals, they can then be placed strategically. Providing an appropriate organizational context in which multiculturals can take on the roles that allow their multicultural minds and skills to emerge is the subject of the next chapter.

Summary

As organizations increasingly face knowledge-based competition, they often turn to teams of people to generate the innovative solutions they need. Culturally diverse teams are capable of generating more creative ideas than single culture teams.

Organizations can be a powerful influence on the situation by creating imposed roles or by allowing innate roles to emerge. Multiculturals, because of their broader worldview, higher levels of sensitivity and perceptual acuity, greater empathy, and more complex ways of thinking can function well in a number of organizational and team roles that are important for innovation. In teams they can act as *bridges* across cultural fault lines, as *integrators* of the views of culturally different team members, and as *mediators* by intervening to reduce destructive forms of team conflict. Multiculturals may not excel at all these roles, depending on how they manage their multicultural identities.

Not all teams interact face to face. So-called virtual teams work across geographies primarily through electronic networks. Virtual teams have special challenges in communicating, relationship building, and conflict management, all of which can be handled more easily by multiculturals. Teams exist within the context of the larger organization and can be influenced by organizational strategy, authority structures, and regulations. Multiculturals can engage in important boundary-spanning activities that can have a positive influence on innovation. These activities include *exchanging* information across boundaries, *linking* disconnected organizational units, *facilitating* cross-boundary interactions, and *intervening* to resolve misunderstandings. To leverage these important boundary-spanning skills, organizations must produce a context that allows multiculturals to play out their innate roles.

CHAPTER NINE

THE NEEDS OF THE MANY OUTWEIGH THE NEEDS OF THE FEW

Leveraging the Skills of Multiculturals and Building an Innovative Organization

The quotation in the chapter title is perhaps the most famous line in the history of the television series and movie franchise *Star Trek*.[1] It is of course attributed to Mr. Spock (played by Leonard Nimoy), the pointy eared, green-blooded, half Vulcan and half human first officer of the starship *Enterprise*. Spock, like the multicultural people discussed in this book,[2] was constantly forced to confront his multicultural identity. Spock's difference forced his culturally diverse crewmates to be self-aware and to examine their own assumptions about the way in which their own cultural programing influenced their perspectives. Spock often demonstrated his skills in boundary spanning between the crew of the *Enterprise* and the alien species of the moment. Also, their organization, the *Enterprise,* was an environment that got the best, not only from the multicultural and ever so logical Spock but also from the mercurial Captain Kirk, not to mention Sulu, Chekov, Uhura, and a cornucopia of crew members from the far reaches of the planet and the galaxy. While the *Enterprise* operated within the confines of the defined rules of its parent organization, Starfleet, the flexible situation on board the starship allowed the creativity that was often required to deal with the many unexpected encounters of space exploration.

Creating an innovative organization involves recognizing as a valuable asset the cultural diversity that exists within individuals, like Mr. Spock, in the same way that we have come to treat the cultural diversity between individuals. These individuals, who are often marginalized, must be integrated into the knowledge sharing and decision systems of the organization. It also means that training and development programs should focus on modeling the multicultural experience so that everyone in the organization can develop the mental skills to be more creative. This concluding chapter sums up the organizational interventions that, based on an understanding of multiculturals, engages them, leverages their unique skills and abilities, and models their development in the organization.

> The best way to guarantee a steady stream of new ideas is to make sure that each person in your organization is as different as possible from the others. Under these conditions, and only these conditions, will people maintain varied perspectives and demonstrate their knowledge in different ways. (Nick Negroponte, Greek American founder of MIT Media Lab)
>
> You never know where the next innovation will come from. New ideas can circle the globe in an instant.
>
> True innovation, we have found, comes from this beautiful fusion of cultures, ideas, beliefs, and experiences. (Muhtar Kent, Turkish American CEO of Coca Cola Company)[3]
>
> Diverse and unexpected pools of talent are emerging around the world. To succeed in today's global economy, we must

acknowledge them, understand them, and make them part of our talent strategies. (Bob Moritz, US chairman and senior partner, PricewaterhouseCoopers)

The principles for achieving innovation are not a secret,[4] but the secret weapon in leveraging today's culturally diverse workforce for innovation may be the multicultural mind. The creativity of individuals and teams, combined with a supportive organizational climate, is the key to innovation. Multiculturals, with their unique skills, are an underutilized resource in today's multicultural organizations. Effectively utilizing the skills of multicultural individuals requires that organizations engage with them effectively.

Engaging Multiculturals

Like Spock, multiculturals are sensitive to the fact they are different. They will be looking for organizations where their multicultural background is valued. Organizations seeking to attract multicultural individuals must create visible signs of an inclusive environment. And, of course, to retain them this expectation that the organization creates in new employees must turn out to be the reality. The recognition that organizations cannot succeed without managing diversity, and that it leads to innovation, is apparent in the following statements from the websites of several industry leaders.

> *IBM:* IBM's enduring commitment to diversity is one of the reasons we can credibly say that IBM is one of the world's leading globally integrated enterprises. We also understand that diversity goes beyond fair hiring practices and protection for all employees. It also includes a focus on how those disparate pieces

fit together to create an innovative, integrated whole. We call this approach "inclusion."

While our differences shape who we are as individual IBMers, our shared corporate culture and values remain central to our mutual success. IBMers around the world work in an environment where diversity—including diversity of thought—is the norm, which yields a commitment to creating client innovation in every part of our business.[5]

Apple: At Apple, our 98,000 employees share a passion for products that change people's lives, and from the very earliest days we have known that diversity is critical to our success. We believe deeply that inclusion inspires innovation.

Our definition of diversity goes far beyond the traditional categories of race, gender, and ethnicity. It includes personal qualities that usually go unmeasured, like sexual orientation, veteran status, and disabilities. Who we are, where we come from, and what we've experienced influence the way we perceive issues and solve problems. We believe in celebrating that diversity and investing in it.[6]

Cisco Systems: Today's organizations face increasing demands for responsiveness, adaptability, innovation, speed, and responsible corporate citizenship. No organization can afford to dismiss the potential benefits of having a diverse and inclusive culture.

So for Cisco, building an inclusive and diverse organization is an ongoing and essential business imperative. We truly believe it is our responsibility to:

Empower our teams

Eliminate biases

Create an environment where everyone feels welcomed, valued, respected, and heard.[7]

The idea of creating a positive climate for diversity is not new, but it is as important in attracting, engaging, and motivating multiculturals as it is in a diverse workforce overall. It is an umbrella under which all organizational policies operate.

Providing an environment in which multiculturals will be engaged in the process of innovation goes well beyond just creating a positive climate for diversity. Engaging multiculturals in a way that their natural talents will emerge involves promoting an organizational culture that creates *flexible situations,* fosters *strong communication*, and provides *sufficient resources.*

Flexible Situations. Organizations can have a dramatic influence on the way their members think, feel, and act. In order to engage multiculturals in the process of innovation, organizations need to promote flexible situations, as opposed to strong situations. Strong situations are created by policies, procedures, and norms for behavior that prescribe what is expected (recall the guards and prisoners in the Stanford Prison Experiment). These situations will stifle the expression of the roles that feel natural to multicultural individuals and suppress their skills and abilities. What is needed for the expression of creativity and for the talents of multiculturals to emerge is an organizational culture that allows unofficial activity, that encourages tinkering and experimentation, and that recognizes the role that serendipity plays. Organizations that encourage members to take risks must also have a tolerance for failure. To evaluate the culture of your organization, ask yourself the following questions:

- Does your organization have a rigid organizational structure?
- Is unofficial activity legitimate? How do managers react if employees engage in activity outside their job descriptions?

- Does your organization have policies or practices that prevent members from taking risks? Are there strong sanctions for failure?

- Is there a strong sense of the type of behavior that is "appropriate" in the organization? Is there one best way to do things?

- Does your organization have a climate of inclusion in which everyone feels valued and respected?

Strong Communication. Innovation in organizations requires the free exchange of information. Strong communication that supports innovation involves messages sent by top management as well as communication across organizational units and among members from different cultures. Strong communication begins with top management sending the message that the organization has an orientation toward innovation and that all organization members have equal status in that process. Since it is impossible to predict where the next novel idea will come from, everyone in the organization needs to feel that they have a stake in the creative process and that their ideas are just as good as anyone else's ideas. The channels through which to share these ideas need to be open to them. Filling the organization with multiculturals does no good if they don't fully participate in roles that are consistent with their skills. Organization members who feel that they will not be understood or that their ideas will not be valued will not be motivated to engage. This is particularly critical in multicultural workforces where a significant number of employees may be less than fully fluent in the corporate language (typically English). In order to perform their boundary-spanning roles, multiculturals need open communication channels to the broader organization. How strong is the communications climate in your organization?

- Are you confident that novel ideas are brought to the surface and widely discussed? Does everyone in the organization know the expertise of other organization members?

- Does your organization have an effective system (either formal or informal) for communicating across cultural (language) groups, across organizational units, upward to top management?

- Is it clear that requests from other organization members for information should be given a high priority no matter where they come from?

- Are informal groups of people who have a common interest encouraged? Are there ways for people who don't normally interact to come together?

- Do all employees feel comfortable in expressing themselves in the language in which they feel most comfortable?

- Does your organization have a climate of inclusion where everyone feels their ideas are valued and respected?

Sufficient Resources. Individuals and teams cannot innovate without the minimally sufficient resources to complete their tasks. However, simply throwing resources at problems may not be the best way to create an engaging environment for multiculturals. Sometimes the most innovative solutions occur when individuals are making do with what is at hand and are forced to consider alternative solutions. This often requires different paths to the desired organizational goals. It is important to recognize that in culturally diverse environments, a key resource is time. Multicultural groups and teams, while often providing superior solutions, typically take longer to be productive. An additional requirement for getting the most out of multiculturals is access to diverse resources. One of the talents of multicultural individuals is their ability to generate novel ideas. However, they have numerous other roles to play in getting the most out of a culturally diverse workforce. Are sufficient resources available to multiculturals in your organization?

- Do all employees have a good understanding of how to acquire the resources they need?
- Is time flexibility built into project plans?
- Do managers and team leaders have operational flexibility in achieving organizational goals?
- Are teams and workgroups made up of culturally diverse and diversely skilled individuals?
- Does your organization have a climate of inclusion where everyone understands, values, and respects others?

Motivating Innovation

One of the most consistent findings in research on creativity is that people are more creative when they are doing work that they find interesting (intrinsically motivating).[8] Unsurprisingly, multiculturals are most likely to contribute to innovation when they are engaged in work that they love and in roles in which they feel comfortable. We have long known how to create work that is intrinsically motivating;[9] it involves designing jobs that have high levels of autonomy, require a variety of skills, and have meaningful outcomes. To get the best out of multicultural employees, the organization needs to assign them complex and challenging (but achievable) tasks that require the use of their unique skills.[10] They will excel on tasks that require their broader worldview, higher sensitivity and perceptual acuity, greater empathy, and ability to engage in more complex thinking to problems. They will then be excited about their work and interested in completing tasks without external controls or constraints. Assigning multiculturals to relatively simple and routine tasks, or tasks with unrealistic expectations, will be unlikely to yield the kind of innovation organizations are seeking. Because of the difficulty of matching multicultural individuals to tasks, it may be necessary to rotate them through a number of assignments until a good fit is found.

The contribution of multiculturals to the process of innovation is also influenced by the way in which they are supervised.[11] Controlling supervision in which employee behavior is closely monitored and employees feel pressure to conform has a negative effect on innovation. In contrast, supportive supervision in which employees are encouraged to speak up about their ideas and concerns, and which provides positive informal feedback, encourages multiculturals to assume roles that feel natural to them and that will support innovation. So it's not just doing what you love that is important to innovation; it is also being allowed by your organization to do what you love.

Developing Multicultural Minds

There are two aspects to developing multicultural minds in the service of innovation within organizations. First, multiculturals are often unaware of their special skills and abilities. So it is important not only to create an environment that allows these skills to emerge but also to provide feedback mechanisms to multiculturals about their performance in specific roles. It is critically important that this feedback be developmental as opposed to evaluative. It should focus on:

- Helping multiculturals understand and develop their skills

- Diagnosing any individual or organizational problems that are hindering their creative performance

- Enhancing their commitment through recognition for their performance

Second, instead of relying solely on the existing pool of multiculturals in the organization (or those who can be recruited in the short term) as the engines of creativity, a longer-term solution to improving innovation is to develop more multicultural minds in the organization. The question then becomes, Can we create multicultural minds by designing development activities that model the way in which multiculturals develop their special skills? The answer lies in understanding how the multicultural mind develops. As discussed in chapter 3, the final stage of multicultural development is the conscious consideration of one's own values, attitudes, beliefs, and assumptions about appropriate behavior in contrast with people who are culturally different. In order to resolve these differences, we must become aware of them, consider the merits of alternative perspectives, and form reasonable trade-offs between them. Resolving these differences is how the multicultural mind is formed. The multicultural mind is created by transforming our experiences with people who are culturally different into knowledge and more complex ways of thinking.[12]

Many organizations offer the day-to-day contact with people who are culturally different that is needed to develop a multicultural mind. This contact includes overseas assignments, cross-cultural teams, and interaction with people who are culturally different at home.

> You can get some good multicultural management skills by working on international projects inside many organizations, even if you are based in your own country. Some people are mobile to go abroad, some people are not. If you are not, because you have family constraints or health constraints or for whatever reason, you can still have international exposure and a multicultural experience by working on a project which involves people from other countries, or involves people in different companies. You can be based in Paris and have a job in which you only work with French people, and only with French people who are engineers and who went to the same school as you did. Or you could be in Paris, sitting at your own desk but working with colleagues who are Russian, Japanese, or Brazilian, working with people from sales and finance and engineering, and communication. I would encourage people to take these types of challenging assignments—those that have international flavor and cross-cultural contact. . . . The key point is to get people out of their comfort zone, learn new languages, travel to different countries, go to places where you don't understand the culture, and expose yourself to situations where you have to deal with uncertainty. All of this helps you put yourself in the shoes of people who are different from you. (Carlos Ghosn, chairman of Renault–Nissan Alliance) [13]

Not all contact with other cultures results in the required mental development. These experiences need to provide the opportunity for deep reflection on culturally different meaning systems. Based on the simple idea that people learn the most from doing things they have not done before, we have long known that challenging experiences produce the most learning. Based on the optimal contact strategy discussed in chapter 6, we know that positive effects of contact between dissimilar groups occur when they are involved in an active goal-oriented effort. However, these types of situations come with the risk of failure, which must be managed.

A temporary period of living and working in a foreign country provides an opportunity for the intense experiential learning required to develop a multicultural mind. Recent research shows that international assignees show the kind of mental development required in as little as one year.[14] However, the typical expatriate assignment is often much more concerned with accomplishing some task or with exerting control over a foreign subsidiary than it is with development of the individual.[15] Programs that include all the requirements for the development of a multicultural mind are the global experiential programs used by some leading companies, in which high-potential employees work in multicultural groups to solve problems in developing countries. An example is Project Ulysses at PricewaterhouseCoopers.

PricewaterhouseCoopers (PwC) consists of legally independent firms in 150 countries and employs more than 160,000 people (5 percent of whom are partners). Project Ulysses is an integrated service learning program initiated by PwC in 2001. It involves sending participants in teams to developing countries to work with NGOs, social entrepreneurs, or international organizations. These multicultural teams of three to four people work on a pro bono basis in field assignments for eight weeks helping communities deal with the effects of poverty, conflict, and environmental degradation. As of 2008, 120 PwC partners from 35 different countries had participated in the program. The overall goal of the project was to develop global leaders in PwC's world-wide network of firms. In reporting on the leadership needs of PwC, Ralf Schneider, a PwC partner based in Frankfurt and head of global talent development said, "It was clear it was not going to be a standard business model with a standard leader. We needed to take people outside of that box." Knowledge gained by individuals is transferred back to the organization not only as participants resume their jobs but also through formal debriefing sessions; that knowledge permits PwC to continuously refine the Ulysses model.

Examples of project teams are the following:

Brian McCann, a PwC client service partner from Boston who specializes in mergers and acquisitions, was the only US member of the 2003 Belize team that included colleagues from Malaysia, Sweden, and Germany. Their mission was to work with Ya'axche Conservation Trust to evaluate the growth and income-generating potential of the ecotourism market in southern Belize, where 50 percent of the population is unemployed, and 75 percent earn less than US$200 a month. Brian reported that the learning experience from both a personal and a professional perspective was profound.

Dinu Bumbacea, a PwC partner from Romania, and his teammates from Thailand, Australia, and the United Kingdom worked with the Elias Mutale Training Centre in Kasama, Zambia, along with the United Nations Development Program and Africare on a strategy for economic diversification in the region. Dinu said that the experience gave him new insight into operating in a multicultural environment and team and in dealing with the public sector.[16]

An independent assessment of the outcomes of the project was conducted with 70 participants approximately two years after they returned. The results indicated the participants had developed knowledge and skills similar to those held by multiculturals.[17] They had multicultural minds!

Ulysses and similar programs incorporate all the activities that model the way in which the multicultural mind develops. These programs present an experience similar to the subconscious and involuntary way in which multiculturals have learned about and ultimately internalized more than one cultural meaning system. Through this significant exposure to other cultures and to colleagues from other cultures, they will develop the broader world view, higher levels of sensitivity and perceptual acuity, greater empathy, and more complex ways of thinking that make up the multicultural mind.

Summary

The principles for achieving innovation in organizations are well known. However, what is less well recognized is that the key to leveraging today's culturally diverse workforce for innovation is the multicultural mind. Unleashing the skills of multiculturals requires recognizing the cultural diversity that exists within individuals in the same way we have come to treat cultural diversity between people as an asset. Creativity is the first step in innovation, and the multicultural mind is more creative. However, for creativity to result in innovation, novel ideas must be implemented. The unique skills of multiculturals lend themselves to important roles that support innovation both in teams and in the larger organization. Because it is difficult to understand the specific talents of any single multicultural individual, organizations are best advised to try to attract a wide range of multicultural individuals and create an environment that allows them to assume roles that feel natural to them. Engaging and motivating multiculturals includes creating a positive climate for diversity. It also means designing intrinsically motivating jobs and promoting an organizational culture that creates *flexible situations,* fosters *strong communication,* and provides *sufficient resources.* Developing multicultural minds in the organization involves making multiculturals aware of their unique skills and abilities. It also means developing more multicultural minds in the organization, through well-thought-out experiential programs that model the way in which the multicultural mind develops in multicultural individuals. More multicultural minds mean more opportunity for innovation. By modeling the multicultural experience, we can all develop a multicultural mind.

NOTES

Chapter 1

    1. See Benet-Martínez & Hong, 2014, for a compilation of the most recent academic research on multicultural identity.

    2. Population Division of the United Nations Secretariat, 2011.

    3. Hamel, 2000.

    4. According to *iSixSigma* (iSixSima.com), "Six Sigma is a disciplined, data-driven approach and methodology, developed by Motorola in 1986, for eliminating defects (driving toward six standard deviations between the mean and the nearest specification limit) in any process."

    5. The Conference Board, 2015.

    6. See Amabile, 1997, for a discussion of the componential theory of individual creativity.

    7. Amabile, 1993.

    8. Meehan, 2013.

    9. The first sentence is a common definition of creativity in psychology; the second is from Osho, 1999.

    10. See Diego Rodriguez's influential blog *metacool*.

    11. Amabile, 1993.

    12. From Johnson, 2010; Guier & Weiffenbach, 1997.

13. Maddux & Galinsksy, 2009. See also Chang et al., 2014.

14. Duncker, 1945.

15. See Fitzsimmons, 2013.

16. For a summary of research in this area see Thomas & Peterson, 2014.

17. See Phinney, 1999.

18. See Sternberg, 1985.

Chapter 2

1. This story was adapted from Seelye & Wasilewski, 1996.

2. See Barlow, 1991, for a description of the *wero*.

3. See Howard, 1991.

4. See Triandis, 1994.

5. See Bell, 1973; Kahl, 1968, for a more complete discussion.

6. Yang, 1988.

7. See Watson, 1997, for additional discussion.

8. American is used here in the colloquial sense to mean people living in the United States, recognizing that everyone in the Americas can properly be called Americans.

9. See Osland & Bird, 2000.

10. For a discussion see Nisbett et al., 2001.

11. Bryant & Law, 2004.

12. Global Commission on International Migration, 2005.

13. Abstracted from Roy, 2014.

14. Meet young immigrants, *Scholastic*, accessed July 17, 2015, http://teacher.scholastic.com/activities/immigration/young_immigrants/vandi.htm.

15. Lindsay, 2014.

16. See Triandis, 1995, for a discussion.

17. See Berry, 1997, for more on acculturation.

18. Kosic et al., 2004.

19. See Oberg, 1960, for a full description of this effect.

20. From Thomas & Inkson, 2009.

21. This metaphor is typically attributed to E. T. Hall, 1976.

Chapter 3

1. From Gladwell, 1998.

2. For a thorough discussion of self-identity, see Markus, 1977; Markus & Kitayama, 1991.

3. See Hamaguchi, 1985.

4. See Kitayama & Uskul, 2011.

5. From Bontempo, Lobel & Triandis, 1990.

6. From Pekerti & Thomas, 2015.

7. Liu, 1998.

8. See Tajfel, 1981.

9. See Ashforth & Mael, 1989.

10. See Hong et al., 2000.

11. As discussed in chapter 4, frame switching is not uniform among multiculturals. See also Benet-Martínez et al., 2002.

12. This discussion draws heavily on Tadmor & Tetlock, 2006.

13. This stage model should not be overinterpreted. It is presented for illustration only. Individuals may not pass sequentially through these stages. And there may be no clear demarcation between the stages.

14. Adapted from Pekerti & Thomas, 2015. Recent research on *brain plasticity* shows that both the structure and function of the human brain can be reorganized as a result of environmental factors. See, for example, Maguire et al., 1999.

15. See Tetlock, 1986, and Tetlock et al., 1996, for a discussion.

16. See, for example, Piaget, 1929; Erikson, 1993.

17. Deloch-Hughes, 2012.

18. See the excellent book by Pollock & Van Reken, 2009, for a comprehensive discussion of TCKs.

19. See Lee, Bain & McCallum, 2007, for an interesting study of creativity in TCKs.

Chapter 4

1. These quotations are from an unpublished study by Fitzsimmons, Vora & Thomas, 2015.

2. For more on bicultural integration, see work by Verónica Benet-Martínez, especially Benet-Martínez & Haritatos, 2005.

3. This framework is from Fitzsimmons, 2013.

4. From Fitzsimmons, Liao & Thomas, 2015.

5. See Uz, 2015, for an index of tight and loose cultures around the world.

6. From Fitzsimmons, Liao & Thomas, 2015.

7. From Fitzsimmons, Liao & Thomas, 2015.

8. Abstracted from a story in Benet-Martínez & Hong, 2014.

9. From Fitzsimmons, Liao & Thomas, 2015.

10. For more about the self-concept see Markus, 1977, and Markus & Kitayama, 1991.

11. From Thúy, 1998.

12. See Molinsky, 2007, for a discussion of the psychological toll associated with multiple identities.

13. See Shi & Lu, 2007.

14. This perspective on social capital is from Nahapiet & Ghoshal, 1998.

15. Hong & Doz, 2013.

16. Bagby, 1957.

17. For more on this process, see Thomas & Peterson, 2014.

18. See Maguire et al., 2000.

19. See Tadmor & Tetlock, 2006.

20. See Tadmor et al., 2012.

21. For more, see Hong & Doz, 2013.

Chapter 5

1. A sea chantey (pronounced shanty) is derived from the French word *chant* (song). It is a type of work song that was once commonly sung to accompany hard labor on board large merchant ships.

2. Seelye & Wasilewski, 1996.

3. Based on "Rakuten's English policy: Just speak it," *Wall Street Journal Japan*, June 29, 2012.

4. For more on English as a common corporate language, see Neeley, 2012, and Zander et al., 2011.

5. See Zander et al., 2011, for a discussion.

6. See Neeley, 2013, for more on this effect.

7. Adapted from Neeley, 2013.

8. See Friedriksson et al., 2006.

9. See Zander et al., 2011.

10. Thomas, 1999.

11. See Maclean, 2006.

12. Engholm, 1991.

13. As reported in the online newspaper *Nettavisen*.

14. From Hong & Doz, 2013.

15. For more on translation of concrete and abstract words by multiculturals, see Ringberg et al., 2010.

16. These two quotations are from Harzing et al., 2011.

17. From Barner-Rasmussen et al., 2014.

18. For more on this trend, see Marschan-Piekkari et al., 1999.

Chapter 6

1. Race is not really a physical category but a social construction (see Montagu, 1942). Realizing the inadequacy of the term, I (like many scholars) use it here as shorthand to refer to genetically induced variation in humans.

2. Adapted from a story in Seelye & Wasilewski, 1996.

3. From Gaskins, 1999.

4. From Gaskins, 1999.

5. Abstracted from Metchie, 2009.

6. See Wilder, 1978.

7. Adapted from Shaw, 1990.

8. See Smith et al., 2013.

9. Liu, 1998.

10. Early research in this area was conducted by Katz & Braly, 1933.

11. See Sidanius, 1993.

12. Women's Executive Network, 2012.

13. See Benet-Martínez, Leu & Lee, 2006, for more on this effect.

14. Linville & Jones, 1980.

15. See Bandura, 1977.

16. From Sherif, 1966.

17. See Allport, 1954.

18. This is based on an idea first presented in Pettigrew, 1998.

19. See Sagiv & Schwartz, 1995; Patchen, 1982.

Chapter 7

1. From Milgram, 1963.

2. See Peters & Waterman, 1982.

3. See Leung & Chiu, 2010.

4. Bloomberg Business, 2006.

5. See Amabile, 1997, for a discussion.

6. This is an often-told story of dubious authenticity that illustrates findings by Deci, 1972, about intrinsic motivation.

7. See Amabile et al., 1996.

8. From Hackman & Oldham, 1980.

9. Oldham & Cummings, 1996.

10. Adapted from Robinson & Stern, 1997.

11. Office Snapshots, 2015.

12. See Garcia & Hoelscher, 2010.

13. See Cox, 2001, for an extended discussion.

14. The quotations are from Fitzsimmons, Vora & Thomas, 2014.

Chapter 8

1. Strauch, 2010, and the NTSB as reported in Thomas & Peterson, 2014.

2. For a complete description of the experiment, see "The Stanford Prison Experiment," at www.prisonexp.org.

3. See Haney, Banks & Zimbardo, 1973.

4. From a speech in 2008 on accepting the Transcultural Leader Award at INSEAD. Reported in Fitzsimmons, Miska & Stahl, 2011.

5. See Stahl, Maznevski, Voigt & Jonsen, 2010, for a review.

6. See Tadmor, Satterstrom, Jang & Polzer, 2012, for an example.

7. For a more in-depth discussion of cultural diversity in teams, see chapter 8 in Thomas & Peterson, 2014.

8. Lau & Murnighan, 1998; 2005

9. See Galinsksy et al., 2008.

10. Janis, 1982.

11. See Jehn & Mannix, 2001.

12. Karambayya & Brett, 1989.

13. Tinsley, 1998.

14. Adapted from a case in Thomas & Inkson, 2009.

15. Jang, 2014.

16. See Jonsen, Maznevski & Davison, 2012, for a deeper discussion of virtual teams.

17. See Hoegl, Gibbert & Mazursky, 2008; Baker & Nelson, 2005.

18. Barner-Rasmussen et al., 2014.

Chapter 9

1. From *Star Trek II: The Wrath of Khan*, 1982.

2. In 1968 Leonard Nimoy, as Mr. Spock, wrote a long and thoughtful response to a young mixed-race girl who felt she would never fit in. The full exchange can be found at Demby, 2015.

3. From speeches at Columbia University, 2009, and the Colorado Innovation Summit, 2012. According to the company's website, "Coca-Cola boasts six research & development centers, the goal of which is to advance local and regional innovations. The company also has a multicultural, multiethnic, multigenerational innovation council that meets quarterly to develop promising ideas."

4. See Amabile, 1997, for a thorough discussion of these principles of creativity.

5. IBM's website: http://www-03.ibm.com/employment/us/diverse/index.shtml.

6. Apple's website: https://www.apple.com/diversity/.

7. Cisco Systems' website: http://www.cisco.com/web/about/ac49/ac55/about_us.html.

8. Amabile, 1997.

9. Hackman & Oldham, 1980.

10. See Locke & Latham, 1990.

11. Oldham & Cummings, 1996.

12. See Kolb, 1984, for a complete discussion of experiential learning.

13. From an interview in Stahl & Brannen, 2013.

14. Fee, Gray & Lu, 2013.

15. See Thomas & Lazarova, 2014.

16. From *Global Giving Matters*, September–October 2004; Pless, Maak & Stahl, 2011; and PwC's website.

17. Pless, Maak & Stahl, 2011.

BIBLIOGRAPHY

Allport, G. W. (1954). *The nature of prejudice*. Cambridge, MA: Addison-Wesley.

Amabile, T. (1997). Motivating creativity in organizations. *California Management Review*, 40(1), 39–58.

Amabile, T. M. (1993). Motivational synergy: Toward new conceptualizations of intrinsic and extrinsic motivation in the workplace. *Human Resource Management Review*, 3(3), 185–201.

Amabile, T. M., Conti, R., Coon, H., Lazenby, J., & Herron, M. (1996). Assessing the work environment for creativity. *Academy of Management Journal*, 39(5), 1154–1184.

Ashforth, B. E., & Mael, F. (1989). Social identity theory and the organization. *Academy of Management Review*, 14(1), 20–39.

Bagby, J. W. (1957). A cross-cultural study of perceptual predominance in binocular rivalry. *The Journal of Abnormal and Social Psychology*, 54(3), 331.

Baker, T., & Nelson, R. E. (2005). Creating something from nothing: Resource construction through entrepreneurial bricolage. *Administrative Science Quarterly*, 50(3), 329–366.

Bandura, A. (1977). *Social learning theory*. Englewood Cliffs, NJ: Prentice-Hall.

Barlow, C. (1991). *Tikanga whakaaro: Key concepts in Maori culture*. Auckland: Oxford University Press.

Barner-Rasmussen, W., Ehrnrooth, M., Koveshnikov, A., & Mäkelä, K. (2014). Cultural and language skills as resources for boundary spanning within the MNC. *Journal of International Business Studies*, 45(7), 886–905.

Bell, D. (1973). *The coming of the post-industrial society*. New York: Basic Books.

Benet-Martínez, V., & Haritatos, J. (2005). Bicultural identity integration (BII): Components and psychosocial antecedents. *Journal of Personality*, 73(4), 1015–1050.

Benet-Martínez, V., & Hong, Y-Y., eds. (2014). *The Oxford handbook of multicultural identity*. Oxford: Oxford University Press.

Benet-Martínez, V., Lee, F., & Leu, J. (2006). Biculturalism and cognitive complexity expertise in cultural representations. *Journal of Cross-Cultural Psychology*, 37(4), 386–407.

Benet-Martínez, V., Leu, J., Lee, F., & Morris, M. W. (2002). Negotiating biculturalism cultural frame switching in biculturals with oppositional versus compatible cultural identities. *Journal of Cross-Cultural Psychology*, 33(5), 492–516.

Berry, J. W. (1997). Immigration, acculturation, and adaptation. *Applied Psychology: An International Review*, 46(1), 5–34.

Black, J. S., & Mendenhall, M. (1989). A practical but theory-based framework for selecting cross-cultural training methods. *Human Resource Management*, 28(4), 511–539.

Bloomberg Business. (2006). Inside Google's new-product process, June 29, 2006.

Bontempo, R., Lobel, S., & Triandis, H. (1990). Compliance and value internalization in Brazil and the US: Effects of allocentrism and anonymity. *Journal of Cross-Cultural Psychology*, 21(2), 200–213.

Brannen, M. Y., & Thomas, D. C. (2010). Bicultural individuals in organizations: Implications and opportunity. *International Journal of Cross Cultural Management*, 10(1), 5–16.

Bryant, J., & Law, D. (2004). *New Zealand's diaspora and overseas-born population* (No. 04/13). Wellington: New Zealand Treasury.

Chang, J.-H., Hsu, C.-C., Shih, N.-H., & Chen, H.-C. (2014). Multicultural families and creative children. *Journal of Cross-Cultural Psychology*, 45(8), 1288–1296.

The Conference Board of Canada. (2015). Innovation Defined. The Conference Board of Canada, accessed July 13, 2015. http://www.conferenceboard.ca/cbi/innovation.aspx.

Cox Jr, T. (2001). *Creating the multicultural organization: A strategy for capturing the power of diversity.* San Francisco: Jossey-Bass.

Deci, E. L. (1972). Intrinsic motivation, extrinsic reinforcement, and inequity. *Journal of Personality and Social Psychology*, 22(1), 113.

Deloch-Hughes, E. (2012). "Black is beautiful" 50 year anniversary: A movement that went viral before digital technology. *Black Copy*, March 1, 2012.

Demby, G. (2015). Leonard Nimoy's advice to a biracial girl in 1968. Code Switch. February 27, 2015. http://www.npr.org/blogs/codeswitch/2015/02/27/389589676/leonard-nimoys-advice-to-a-biracial-girl-in-1968.

Duncker, K. (1945). On problem solving. *Psychological Monographs*, 58 (5, Serial # 270).

Engholm, C. (1991). *When business East meets business West: The guide to practice and protocol in the Pacific Rim.* New York: John Wiley.

Erikson, E. H. (1993). *Childhood and society.* W. W. Norton & Company.

Fee, A., Gray, S. J., & Lu, S. (2013). Developing cognitive complexity from the expatriate experience: Evidence from a longitudinal field study. *International Journal of Cross Cultural Management*, 13(3), 299–318.

Ferraro, G. P. (2006). *The cultural dimension of international business.* Englewood Cliffs, NJ: Prentice-Hall.

Fitzsimmons, S. R. (2013). Multicultural employees: A framework for understanding how they contribute to organizations. *Academy of Management Review*, 38(4), 491–502.

Fitzsimmons, S. R., Liao, Y., & Thomas, D. C. (2015). From crossing cultures to straddling them: An empirical examination of outcomes for multicultural employees. Manuscript under review.

Fitzsimmons, S. R., Miska, C., & Stahl, G. K. (2011). Multicultural employees: Global business' untapped resource. *Organizational Dynamics*, 40(3), 199–206.

Fitzsimmons, S. R., Vora, D., & Thomas, D. C. (2014). Multicultural employees and culture brokering: Multi-level determinants of brokering behavior. Unpublished manuscript.

Fredriksson, R., Barner-Rasmussen, W., & Piekkari, R. (2006). The multinational corporation as a multilingual organization: The notion of a common corporate language. *Corporate Communications: An International Journal*, 11(4), 406–423.

Galinsky, A. D., Magee, J. C., Gruenfeld, D. H., Whitson, J. A., & Liljenquist, K. A. (2008). Power reduces the press of the situation: Implications for creativity, conformity, and dissonance. *Journal of Personality and Social Psychology*, 95(6), 1450.

Garcia, J. E., & Hoelscher, K. J. (2010). *Managing diversity flashpoints in higher education*. Washington, DC: Rowman & Littlefield Publishers.

Gaskins, P. F. (1999). *What are you? Voices of mixed-race young people*. New York: Henry Holt and Co.

Gladwell, M. (1998). Lost in the middle. In C. Chiawei Oheran (ed.), *Half and half: Writers on growing up biracial and bicultural*. New York: Pantheon Books.

Global Commission on International Migration (2005). Migration in an interconnected world: New directions for action. Global Forum for Migration & Development. http://www.gfmd.org/pfp/ppd/1883.

Guier, W. H., & Weiffenbach, G. C. (1997). Genesis of satellite navigation. *Johns Hopkins APL Technical Digest*, 18(2), 178–181.

Hackman, J. R., & Oldham, G. R. (1980). *Work redesign*, vol. 72. Reading, MA: Addison-Wesley.

Hall, E. T. (1976). *Beyond culture*. New York: Doubleday.

Hamaguchi, E. (1985). A contextual model of the Japanese: Toward a methodological innovation in Japan studies. *Journal of Japanese Studies*, 11(2), 289/321.

Hamel, G. (2000). Reinventing your company, *Fortune*, June 12, 99–118.

Haney, C., Banks, C., & Zimbardo, P. (1973). Interpersonal dynamics in a simulated prison. *International Journal of Criminology and Penology*, 1(1), 69–97.

Harzing, A. W., Köster, K., & Magner, U. (2011). Babel in business: The language barrier and its solutions in the HQ-subsidiary relationship. *Journal of World Business*, 46(3), 279–287.

Hoegl, M., Gibbert, M., & Mazursky, D. (2008). Financial constraints in innovation projects: When is less more? *Research Policy*, 37(8), 1382–1391.

Hong, H., & Doz, Y. (2013). L'Oréal masters multiculturalism. *Harvard Business Review*, 91(6), 114–118.

Hong, Y-Y., Morris, M. W., Chiu, C-Y., & Benet-Martínez, V. (2000). Multicultural minds: A dynamic constructivist approach to culture and cognition. *American Psychologist*, 55, 709–720.

Howard, G. (1991). Culture tales: A narrative approach to thinking, cross-cultural psychology and psychotherapy. *American Psychologist*, 46, 187–197.

Jang, S. (2014). Bringing worlds together: Cultural brokerage in multicultural teams. Unpublished doctoral dissertation. Cambridge, MA: Harvard University.

Janis, I. L. (1982). *Groupthink: Psychological studies of policy decisions and fiascoes*. Boston: Houghton Mifflin.

Jehn, K. A., & Mannix, E. A. (2001). The dynamic nature of conflict: A longitudinal study of intragroup conflict and group performance. *Academy of Management Journal*, 44(2), 238–251.

Johnson, S. (2010). *Where good ideas come from*. New York: Riverhead Press.

Jonsen, K., Maznevski, M. L., & Canney Davison, S. (2012). Global virtual team dynamics and effectiveness. *Handbook of Research in International Human Resource Management*. London: Edward Elgar Publishing.

Kahl, J. A. (1968). *The measure of modernism*. Austin: University of Texas Press.

Karambayya, R., & Brett, J. M. (1989). Managers handling disputes: Third-party roles and perceptions of fairness. *Academy of Management Journal*, 32(4), 687–704.

Katz, D., & Braly, K. (1933). Racial stereotypes of one hundred college students. *The Journal of Abnormal and Social Psychology*, 28(3), 280.

Kitayama, S., & Uskul, A. K. (2011). Culture, mind, and the brain: Current evidence and future directions. *Annual Review of Psychology*, 62, 419–449.

Kolb, D. A. (1984). *Experiential learning: Experience as the source of learning and development.* New Jersey: Prentice-Hall.

Kosic, A., Kruglanski, A. W., Pierro, A., & Mannetti, L. (2004). The social cognition of immigrants' acculturation: Effects of the need for closure and the reference group at entry. *Journal of Personality and Social Psychology,* 86(6), 796.

Lau, D. C., & Murnighan, J. K. (1998). Demographic diversity and faultlines: The compositional dynamics of organizational groups. *Academy of Management Review,* 23(2), 325–340.

Lau, D. C., & Murnighan, J. K. (2005). Interactions within groups and subgroups: The effects of demographic faultlines. *Academy of Management Journal,* 48(4), 645–659.

Lee, Y. J., Bain, S. K., & McCallum, R. S. (2007). Improving creative problem-solving in a sample of third culture kids. *School Psychology International,* 28(4), 449–463.

Leung, A. K. Y., & Chiu, C. Y. (2010). Multicultural experience, idea receptiveness, and creativity. *Journal of Cross-Cultural Psychology,* 41, 723–741.

Lindsay, Daryl. (2014). The new Germans: Immigrant children's complicated search for identity. *SpiegelOnline International,* September 28, 2012. http://www.spiegel.de/international/germany/the-new-germans-three-children-of-immigrants-share-their-stories-a-858563.html.

Linville, P. W., & Jones, E. E. (1980). Polarized appraisals of out-group members. *Journal of Personality and Social Psychology,* 38(5), 689.

Liu, E. (1998). *The accidental Asian: Notes of a native speaker.* New York: Vintage Books.

Locke, E. A., & Latham, G. P. (1990). *A theory of goal setting & task performance.* Prentice-Hall.

Maclean, D. (2006). Beyond English: Transnational corporations and the strategic management of language in a complex multilingual business environment. *Management Decision,* 44(10), 1377–1390.

Maddux, W. W., & Galinsksy, A. D. (2009). Cultural borders and mental barriers: The relationship between living abroad and creativity. *Journal of Personality and Social Psychology,* 96, 1047–1061.

Maguire, E. A., Gadian, D. G., Johnsrude, I. S., Good, C. D.,

Ashburner, J., Frackowiak, R. S., & Frith, C. D. (2000). Navigation-related structural change in the hippocampi of taxi drivers. *Proceedings of the National Academy of Sciences*, 97(8), 4398–4403.

Markus, H. (1977). Self-schemas and processing information about the self. *Journal of Personality and Social Psychology*, 35, 63–78.

Markus, H. R., & Kitayama, S. (1991). Culture and the self: Implications for cognition, emotion, and motivation. *Psychological Review*, 98(2), 224–253.

Marschan-Piekkari, R., Welch, D., & Welch, L. (1999). Adopting a common corporate language: IHRM implications. *International Journal of Human Resource Management*, 10(3), 377–390.

Maznevski, M. L., & Chudoba, K. M. (2000). Bridging space over time: Global virtual team dynamics and effectiveness. *Organization Science*, 11(5), 473–492.

Meehan, M. (2013). Person of Interest: Ruth Handler, Barbie's Creator. *Examiner.com*, November 4, 2013. http://www.examiner.com/article/person-of-interest-ruth-handler-barbie-s-creator.

Metchie, K. (2009). Can't I Just Be Canadian? *The Peak*, Spring 2009.

Milgram, S. (1963). Behavioral study of obedience. *The Journal of Abnormal and Social Psychology*, 67(4), 371.

Molinsky, A. (2007). Cross-cultural code-switching: The psychological challenges of adapting behavior in foreign cultural interactions. *Academy of Management Review*, 32(2), 622–640.

Montagu, M. F. A. (1942). *Man's most dangerous myth: The fallacy of race*. New York: Harper.

Nahapiet, J., & Ghoshal, S. (1998). Social capital, intellectual capital, and the organizational advantage. *Academy of Management Review*, 23(2), 242–266.

Neeley, T. (2012). Global business speaks English: Why you need a language strategy now. *Harvard Business Review*, 90(5), 116–124.

Neeley, T. B. (2013). Language matters: Status loss and achieved status distinctions in global organizations. *Organization Science*, 24(2), 476–497.

Nisbett, R. E., Peng, K., Choi, I., & Norenzayan, A. (2001). Culture and systems of thought: Holistic versus analytic cognition. *Psychological Review*, 108, 291–310.

Oberg, K. (1960). Cultural shock: Adjustment to new cultural environments. *Practical Anthropology, 7,* 177–182.

Office Snapshots. (2015). Pixar Headquarters and the Legacy of Steve Jobs. Accessed July 24, 2015. http://officesnapshots.com/2012/07/16/pixar-headquarters-and-the-legacy-of-steve-jobs/.

Oldham, G. R., & Cummings, A. (1996). Employee creativity: Personal and contextual factors at work. *Academy of Management Journal, 39*(3), 607–634.

Osho. (1999). *Creativity: Unleashing the forces within.* New York: St Martin's Griffin.

Osland, J. S., & Bird, A. (2000). Beyond sophisticated stereotypes: Cultural sensemaking in contex. *Academy of Management Executive, 14,* 65–77.

Patchen, M. (1982). *Black-White contact in schools: Its social and academic effects.* West Lafayette, IN: Purdue University Press.

Pekerti, A. A., & Thomas, D. C. (2015). N-culturals: Modeling the multicultural identity. *Cross-Cultural Management: An International Journal, 15*(10), 5–25.

Pelham, S. D., & Abrams, L. (2014). Cognitive advantages and disadvantages in early and late bilinguals. *Journal of Experimental Psychology: Learning, Memory, and Cognition, 40*(2), 313.

Peters, T. J., & Waterman, R. H. (1982). *In search of excellence.* New York: HarperCollins.

Pettigrew, T. F. (1998). Intergroup contact theory. *Annual Review of Psychology, 49,* 65–85.

Phinney, J. S. (1999). An intercultural approach in psychology: Cultural contact and identity. *Cross-Cultural Psychology Bulletin, 33,* 24–31.

Piaget, J. (1929). *The child's conception of the world* (No. 213). Summit, PA: Rowman & Littlefield.

Pless, N. M., Maak, T., & Stahl, G. K. (2011). Developing responsible global leaders through international service-learning programs: The Ulysses experience. *Academy of Management Learning & Education, 10*(2), 237–260.

Pollock, D. C., & Van Reken, R. E. (2009). *Third culture kids: Growing up among worlds.* Rev. ed. Boston: Nicholas Brealey.

Ringberg, T. V., Luna, D., Reihlen, M., & Peracchio, L. A. (2010).

Bicultural-bilinguals: The effect of cultural frame switching on translation equivalence. *International Journal of Cross Cultural Management*, 10(1), 77–92.

Robinson, A. G., & Stern, S. (1997). *Corporate creativity: How innovation and improvement actually happen.* San Francisco: Berrett-Koehler Publishers.

Roy, B. (2014). Hungarian-born swimmer Zsofia Balazs gives back. *Canadian Immigrant.* May 30, 2014. http://canadianimmigrant.ca/ immigrant-stories/community-immigrant-stories/hungarian-born -swimmer-zsofia-balazs-gives-back.

Sagiv, L., & Schwartz, S. H. (1995). Value priorities and readiness for out-group social contact. *Journal of Personality and Social Psychology,* 69(3), 437.

Seelye, H. N., & Wasilewski, J. H. (1996). *Between cultures: Developing self-identity in a world of diversity.* New York: McGraw-Hill.

Shaw, J. B. (1990). A cognitive categorization model for the study of inter-cultural management. *Academy of Management Review,* 15(4), 626–645.

Sherif, M. (1966). *In common predicament.* Boston: Houghton Mifflin.

Shi, X., & Lu, X. (2007). Bilingual bicultural development of Chinese American adolescents: A comparative study. *Howard Journal of Communications,* 18, 313–333.

Sidanius, J. (1993). The psychology of group conflict and the dynamics of oppression: A social dominance perspective. In S. Iyenger & W. McGuire (eds.), *Explorations in Political Psychology.* Durham, NC: Duke University Press.

Smith, P. B., Fischer, R., Vignoles, V. L., & Bond, M. H. (2013). *Social psychology across cultures: Engaging with a changing world.* London: Sage Publishing.

Stahl, G. K., & Brannen, M. Y. (2013). Building cross-cultural leadership competence: An interview with Carlos Ghosn. *Academy of Management Learning & Education,* 12(3), 494–502.

Stahl, G. K., Maznevski, M. L., Voigt, A., & Jonsen, K. (2010). Unraveling the effects of cultural diversity in teams: A meta-analysis of research on multicultural work groups. *Journal of International Business Studies,* 41(4), 690–709.

Sternberg, R. J. (1985). *Beyond IQ: A triarchic theory of intelligence.* Cambridge: Cambridge University Press.

Strauch, B. (2010). Can cultural differences lead to accidents? Team cultural differences and sociotechnical systems operations. *Human Factors*, 52, 246–263.

Tadmor, C. T., Galinsky, A. D., & Maddux, W. W. (2012). Getting the most out of living abroad: Biculturalism and integrative complexity as key drivers of creative and professional success. *Journal of Personality and Social Psychology*, 103(3), 520.

Tadmor, C. T., Satterstrom, P., Jang, S., & Polzer, J. T. (2012). Beyond individual creativity: The superadditive benefits of multicultural experience for collective creativity in culturally diverse teams. *Journal of Cross-Cultural Psychology*, 43(3), 384–392.

Tadmor, C. T., & Tetlock, P. E. (2006). Biculturalism: A model of the effects of second-culture exposure on acculturation and integrative complexity. *Journal of Cross-Cultural Psychology*, 37(2), 173–190.

Tajfel, H. (1981). *Human groups and social categories.* Cambridge: Cambridge University Press.

Tetlock, P. E. (1986). A value pluralism model of ideological reasoning. *Journal of Personality and Social Psychology*, 50(4), 819.

Tetlock, P. E., Peterson, R. S., & Lerner, J. S. (1996). Revising the value pluralism model: Incorporating social content and context postulates. In C. Seligman, J. M. Olson, & M. P. Zanna (eds.), *The psychology of values: The Ontario symposium*, vol. 9, pp. 25–49. Mahwah, NJ: Lawrence Erlbaum.

Thomas, D. C. (1999). Cultural diversity and work group effectiveness: An experimental study. *Journal of Cross-Cultural Psychology*, 30(2), 242–263.

Thomas, D. C., & Inkson, K. (2009). *Cultural intelligence: Living and working globally.* San Francisco: Berrett-Koehler.

Thomas, D. C., & Lazarova, M. B. (2014). *Essentials of international human resource management: Managing people globally.* Thousand Oaks, CA: Sage.

Thomas, D. C., & Peterson, M. F. (2014). *Cross-cultural management*, 3rd ed. Thousand Oaks, CA: Sage.

Thúy, L. (1998). California palms. In C. Chiawei O'Hearn (ed.), *Half and half: Writers on growing up biracial and bicultural.* New York: Pantheon Books.

Tinsley, C. (1998). Models of conflict resolution in Japanese, German, & American cultures. *Journal of Applied Psychology*, 83(2): 316–323.

Triandis, H. C. (1994). *Culture and social behavior.* New York: McGraw Hill.

Triandis, H. C. (1995). *Individualism and collectivism.* Boulder, CO: Westview.

Uz, I. (2015). The index of cultural tightness and looseness among 68 countries. *Journal of Cross-Cultural Psychology*, 46, 319–335.

Watson, J. L. (1997). *Golden arches east: McDonald's in East Asia.* Stanford, CA: Stanford University Press.

Wilder, D. A. (1978). Reduction of intergroup discrimination through individuation of the out-group. *Journal of Personality and Social Psychology*, 36(12), 1361.

Women's Executive Network. (2013). Conversations with Top 100 Winner: Dr. Amiee Chan. Women's Executive Network, September 23, 2012. https://www.wxnetwork.com/conversations-with-top-100-winner -dr-aimee-chan-2012-corporate-executives-president-ceo-norsat -international/.

Yang, K. S. (1988). Will societal modernization eventually eliminate cross-cultural psychological difference? In M. H. Bond (ed.), *The Cross-Cultural Challenge to Social Psychology.* Newbury Park, CA: Sage.

Zander, L., Mockaitis, A. I., & Harzing, A. W. (2011). Standardization and contextualization: A study of language and leadership across 17 countries. *Journal of World Business*, 46(3), 296–304.

INDEX

ABOUT THE AUTHOR

DAVID C. THOMAS is the Beedie Professor of International Management at Simon Fraser University, Vancouver, Canada, and an Editor of the *Journal of International Business Studies.* He is the author of numerous journal articles and 10 books including (with Kerr Inkson) the best-selling *Cultural Intelligence: Living and Working Globally* (2009, Berrett-Koehler Publishers). His book *Cross-Cultural Management: Essential Concepts* (2008, Sage Publications) was the winner of the R. Wayne Pace Human Resource Development Book of the Year award for 2008. He has lived and worked in New Zealand, Australia, France, Turkey, the United States, and Canada, and he consults widely with business and government agencies on cultural diversity issues. When not writing or teaching, he can be found scraping or varnishing, or sometimes sailing, his 1984 Hans Christian cutter, *Clovelly.*

Also by David C. Thomas, with Kerr Inkson

Cultural Intelligence
Living and Working Globally, Second Edition

Globalization means that managers need to be prepared to do business with people from a wide range of cultures. But it's just not possible to learn the particular customs and traits of every culture you might come into contact with. *Cultural Intelligence* teaches techniques and people skills that will allow you to function effectively in *any* culture. Instead of providing a laundry list of culturally specific dos and don'ts, David Thomas and Kerr Inkson show how to disable your "cultural cruise control" and pay attention, in a mindful and creative way, to cues in cross-cultural situations. Over time you'll develop a repertoire of skills appropriate to different intercultural settings and will be able to choose the right ones for any given interaction. Illustrated throughout with real-life stories depicting what is and is not culturally intelligent behavior, this second edition applies the concept of cultural intelligence to interactions not just in organizations but also in people's daily lives.

Paperback, 240 pages, ISBN 978-1-57675-625-6
PDF ebook ISBN 978-1-57675-799-4
Digital audio ISBN 978-1-62656-605-7

BK Berrett–Koehler Publishers, Inc.
www.bkconnection.com   **800.929.2929**

Berrett–Koehler
Publishers

Berrett-Koehler is an independent publisher dedicated to an ambitious mission: *connecting people and ideas to create a world that works for all.*

We believe that to truly create a better world, action is needed at all levels—individual, organizational, and societal. At the individual level, our publications help people align their lives with their values and with their aspirations for a better world. At the organizational level, our publications promote progressive leadership and management practices, socially responsible approaches to business, and humane and effective organizations. At the societal level, our publications advance social and economic justice, shared prosperity, sustainability, and new solutions to national and global issues.

A major theme of our publications is "Opening Up New Space." Berrett-Koehler titles challenge conventional thinking, introduce new ideas, and foster positive change. Their common quest is changing the underlying beliefs, mindsets, institutions, and structures that keep generating the same cycles of problems, no matter who our leaders are or what improvement programs we adopt.

We strive to practice what we preach—to operate our publishing company in line with the ideas in our books. At the core of our approach is stewardship, which we define as a deep sense of responsibility to administer the company for the benefit of all of our "stakeholder" groups: authors, customers, employees, investors, service providers, and the communities and environment around us.

We are grateful to the thousands of readers, authors, and other friends of the company who consider themselves to be part of the "BK Community." We hope that you, too, will join us in our mission.

A BK Business Book

This book is part of our BK Business series. BK Business titles pioneer new and progressive leadership and management practices in all types of public, private, and nonprofit organizations. They promote socially responsible approaches to business, innovative organizational change methods, and more humane and effective organizations.

Berrett–Koehler
Publishers

Connecting people and ideas
to create a world that works for all

Dear Reader,

Thank you for picking up this book and joining our worldwide community
of Berrett-Koehler readers. We share ideas that bring positive change into
people's lives, organizations, and society.

To welcome you, we'd like to offer you a free e-book. You can pick from
among twelve of our bestselling books by entering the promotional code
BKP92E here: http://www.bkconnection.com/welcome.

When you claim your free e-book, we'll also send you a copy of our e-news-
letter, the *BK Communiqué*. Although you're free to unsubscribe, there are
many benefits to sticking around. In every issue of our newsletter you'll find

- A free e-book
- Tips from famous authors
- Discounts on spotlight titles
- Hilarious insider publishing news
- A chance to win a prize for answering a riddle

Best of all, our readers tell us, "Your newsletter is the only one I actually
read." So claim your gift today, and please stay in touch!

Sincerely,

Charlotte Ashlock
Steward of the BK Website

Questions? Comments? Contact me at bkcommunity@bkpub.com.